EXERCISE IN ACTION

STRENGTH
TRAINING

EXERCISE IN ACTION
STRENGTH TRAINING

Hollis Lance Liebman

THUNDER BAY
P·R·E·S·S
San Diego, California

THUNDER BAY
P·R·E·S·S

Thunder Bay Press
An imprint of the Baker & Taylor Publishing Group
10350 Barnes Canyon Road, San Diego, CA 92121
www.thunderbaybooks.com

All notations of errors or omissions should be addressed to
Thunder Bay Press, Editorial Department, at the above address.
All other correspondence (author inquiries, permissions)
concerning the content of this book should be addressed to
Moseley Road, Inc., 123 Main Street, Irvington, NY 10533.
www.moseleyroad.com.

Library of Congress Cataloging-in-Publication Data

Liebman, Hollis Lance.
  Exercise in action: strength training / Hollis Lance Liebman.
    pages cm.
  ISBN 978-1-62686-053-7 (pbk.) -- ISBN 1-62686-053-X ()
1. Bodybuilding. 2. Weight lifting. 3. Muscle strength. I. Title.
  GV546.5.L47 2014
  613.7'13--dc23
                        2013038539

Printed in China
1 2 3 4 5 18 17 16 15 14

CONTENTS

Introduction

People have been training for strength for thousands of years; the earliest records of stone lifting come from ancient Greece, and sculptures portray various lifting feats. Closer to the present day, the late 19th century saw the appearance of the dumbbell and barbell for use in strength training. Exercise machines appeared in the 1960s, and the following decade introduced us to Arnold Schwarzenegger in the movie *Pumping Iron*, which opened the floodgates of strength training and bodybuilding. It would then enter the mainstream and become the established fitness activity it is today.

Strength training, or resistance training as it now also known, has been used by millions of people who wish to boost their performance levels and physical appearance. It involves using a handheld weight or other form of resistance, which is moved through a specific pathway or motion for a given number of repetitions in order to increase the power output of a specific muscle or muscles. Generally speaking, a muscle that faces an increasing resistance over time will, through ample nutrition and recovery, adapt by growing stronger and bigger.

Many types of athletes and physique enthusiasts perform strength training. While it was once commonly thought that strength training would slow down an athlete and leave him or her muscle-bound, this has since been disproved. Athletes and their coaches the world over know that strength training will make muscles more powerful and allow them to fire with more strength—and through a fuller range of motion and accuracy—than the muscles of those who do not include strength training in their routine.

A power lifter moves the maximum weight possible through very low repetitions. He or she is less concerned with isolating a specific muscle, and more interested in the cohesive working of a system of muscles in order to lift as much weight as possible. This is achieved with force, speed, momentum, and technique.

A bodybuilder, or someone who wishes to showcase maximum detail and development within the musculature, is principally concerned with placing tension on a given muscle without involving ancillary muscles. This is accomplished through pace, consistency, and a slow stretching of the muscle, followed by the explosive completion of a given repetition and full contraction at the top of the movement.

Today, individuals of all physical descriptions include strength training in their fitness programs. While cardiovascular exercise is important for the heart, enhances the metabolism, and increases circulation and blood flow, it is actually less efficient for increasing one's fitness than strength training, which does all this and more.

Only through resistance training can one enhance the shape of one's body and actually change its composition. This is why those obsessed with a number on a scale are only seeing part of the big picture. What is the actual body-fat percentage of the individual? What is the lean muscle mass? What is the breakdown of the information provided by the weight, in terms of quality? In terms of muscularity, an upper arm with a 16-inch circumference and little body fat, with a visible vein running through the biceps, will always appear more impressive than a smooth and bloated arm with an 18-inch circumference without a vein in sight. However, in terms of actual strength, the 18-inch arm may indeed have the upper hand; the lean 16-inch arm will, to a large degree, have an absence of visible body fat, which would otherwise be used during lifts as extra cushioning and support. In this regard, the key is to maximize the effects of strength training to not only isolate the muscles, but also to recruit neighboring tissues in order to strengthen the entire body.

This book is split up into sections based on different muscle groups, and contains some of the most effective strengthening exercises in existence for building up each muscle independently. While some modalities or systems, such as kettlebells, tend to be less muscle-isolating and more demanding of multiple tissues, each section is designed to take the practitioner to greater gains and beyond.

In terms of gains and progressions, the suggested upper body repetition ranges generally span from 8 to 10. The range for the lower body is slightly higher, at approximately 10 to 15 repetitions.

Stretches and Warm-Ups

Stretches and warm-ups are very important for the human body. They are as necessary as turning a key in a car's ignition before hitting 65 mph on the open highway. Cold and restricted muscles are less pliable and more susceptible to injury than warm and loose tissue. Nevertheless, try not to overdo it; take a muscle only to its positive threshold in terms of movement and mobility.

Iliotibial Band Stretch

Stretching the iliotibial (IT) band is rather different from stretching other muscles, as the IT band is a thick, fibrous fascia without the elasticity of your muscles. Iliotibial band stretches can make a big difference to back, hip, and knee problems.

TARGET MUSCLES

gluteus maximus

tractus iliotibialis

biceps femoris

semitendinosus

REAR   FRONT

GLUTES AND IT BAND

Step 1 Start in a standing position, and cross your left foot behind your right ankle.

Step 2 Lean forward until you are as close to the floor with your fingertips as you can go. If you are able, grasp your toes, or, as a more difficult modification, place your hands flat on the floor.

Step 3 Hold for 20 seconds and repeat, then switch legs and repeat the entire stretch.

CORRECT ACTION
• Be sure to ease into the movement slowly

AVOID
• Overextending your legs

Rolling Iliotibial Band Stretch

The Rolling Iliotibial (IT) Band Stretch is a variation on the standard IT Band Stretch; a foam roller is used for the routine. Its main benefit is to release tension in the IT band.

Step 1 Lie facedown, supporting your weight on your hands, with your lower body slightly rotated so that your right leg rests on a foam roller situated between your knee and your hip. Cross your left leg over your right thigh; both feet should touch the floor. Keep as much of your weight on the bottom leg while relaxing the other.

Step 2 Roll from your hip to your knee over the foam roller, and hold for 10–30 seconds at the point of greatest release. Switch legs and repeat.

CORRECT ACTION
• Keep your head as still as possible

AVOID
• Rolling on any tender point you may discover during the stretch

TARGET MUSCLES

gluteus maximus

tractus iliotibialis

biceps femoris

vastus lateralis

semitendinosus

REAR   FRONT

GLUTES AND HAMSTRINGS

Glutes Stretch

The Glutes Stretch improves malleability of the main muscle in the buttocks, the gluteus maximus, as well as the smaller gluteus medius and gluteus minimus. These are some of the most important muscles in the body for mobility, so it is vital to keep them stretched and flexible.

Step 1 Lie on your back, with your left leg bent and your foot firmly planted on the ground.

Step 2 Cross your right ankle over your left thigh, resting it just above the kneecap.

Step 3 Reach between your legs to clasp your hands around the left leg and gently pull it toward you, feeling a stretch within the glutes. For a deeper stretch, lift your head off the floor. Hold for 10–30 seconds, then switch legs.

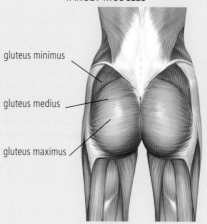

TARGET MUSCLES

gluteus minimus

gluteus medius

gluteus maximus

GLUTES

CORRECT ACTION
• Pull your leg upward slowly

AVOID
• Overextending your neck as you lift your head

Rolling Glutes Stretch

The Rolling Glutes Stretch is a variation on the standard Glutes Stretch. It promotes myofascial release in the glutes, stretching the gluteus maximus and the gluteus medius and minimus muscles above it.

Step 1 Start in a seated position, with a foam roller placed directly beneath your glute muscles. Place your arms behind you for support.

Step 2 Cross your right ankle over your left thigh, shifting your weight to one side.

Step 3 Begin rolling over the belly of the muscle. Hold for 10–30 seconds at the highest point of tension, then switch legs.

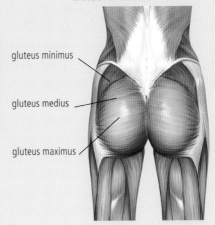

TARGET MUSCLES

gluteus minimus

gluteus medius

gluteus maximus

GLUTES

CORRECT ACTION
- Keep your hands firmly on the floor

AVOID
- Rolling too fast

Lower Back Stretch

This stretch promotes flexibility in the lower back, which is essential for mobility, injury prevention, and to improve performance levels. Though the back is often overlooked as part of a warm-up or cooldown, stretching it will help reduce general muscle aches after an intense workout.

Step 1 Lie on your back with your legs bent.

Step 2 Clasp your hands around your lower legs and pull your knees toward your chest, feeling a deep stretch in the lower back. Hold for 10–30 seconds.

Step 3 Your upper back can also be lifted off the floor to stretch the splenius and cervical portion of the erector spinae.

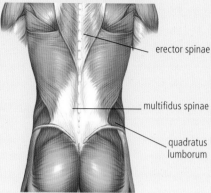

TARGET MUSCLES

erector spinae

multifidus spinae

quadratus lumborum

LOWER BACK

CORRECT ACTION
• Keep your back as straight as possible

AVOID
• Short range of motion
• Overextending your neck if you lift your head

Rolling Lower Back Stretch

The Rolling Lower Back Stretch promotes myofascial release in the erector spinae, relieving tension in the lower section of the back. It also works at the front of the body by strengthening the abdominal muscles.

Step 1 Start in a seated position, with a foam roller placed right behind you. Slowly lower yourself onto the roller, until it is positioned under your lower back. Fold your arms across your chest.

Step 2 Keeping your hips elevated and the tension on your lower back, slowly shift toward one side. Hold this position for 10–30 seconds, then repeat on the other side. Be sure to keep the weight on the muscles, not the spine.

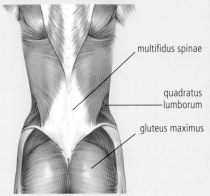

TARGET MUSCLES

multifidus spinae

quadratus lumborum

gluteus maximus

LOWER BACK

CORRECT ACTION
- Keep your feet firmly planted on the floor
- Look for a slow, controlled range of motion

AVOID
- Rolling too far backward
- Overextending your lower back

Seated Spinal Stretch

The Spinal Stretch is an excellent stretch to help free up the spine and relieve the often-constricted erector muscles.

WARNING Those with atrophied lower backs should avoid this exercise.

Step 1 Sit on the floor with one leg stretched out in front of you.

Step 2 Cross your other leg over the outstretched leg, making sure the foot is flat on the ground. Keep one hand on the ground for support and the other placed over your bent leg.

Step 3 Rotate your torso away from the bent leg until your chest is nearly facing the opposite direction from the bent leg.

Step 4 Hold for 30 seconds, repeat, and then switch sides.

CORRECT ACTION
• Keep your back flat at all times

AVOID
• Excessively rotating your torso during the stretch

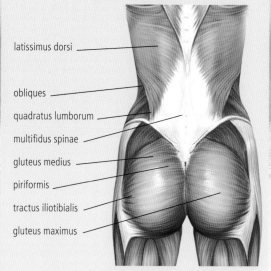

TARGET MUSCLES

latissimus dorsi

obliques

quadratus lumborum

multifidus spinae

gluteus medius

piriformis

tractus iliotibialis

gluteus maximus

BACK

Shoulder Stretch

The Shoulder Stretch is an easy routine that targets the lateral and posterior deltoids. It increases flexibility, mobility, and performance in the upper body, while also helping to relieve tension in the shoulders and neck.

Step 1 Begin in a standing position with your left arm lightly drawn across the front of your body.

Step 2 Bring your right arm underneath your triceps, and gently pull your left arm across the front of your body. Hold for 10–30 seconds, then switch arms.

CORRECT ACTION
- Face forward, keeping your hips perfectly still
- Pull gently at first, increasing slowly

AVOID
- Allowing your upper body to turn
- If you feel any pain, cease immediately

TARGET MUSCLES

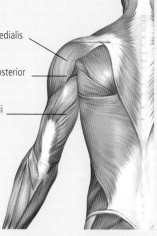

deltoideus medialis

deltoideus posterior

triceps brachii

SHOULDERS

Chest Stretch

The Chest Stretch with your hands clasped behind your head is excellent for stretching the entire chest. It will help to keep your chest muscles flexible.

WARNING Those with atrophied shoulders should avoid this stretch.

Step 1 Begin in a standing position with your hands behind your head, your fingers interlocked, and your elbows pointing outward.

Step 2 Envision expanding the chest outward. Hold for 30 seconds, then move your hands so they meet together in front of you.

Step 3 Relax and repeat for three 30-second holds.

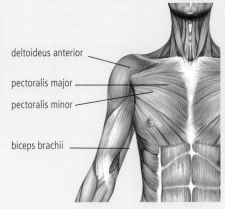

TARGET MUSCLES

deltoideus anterior

pectoralis major

pectoralis minor

biceps brachii

CHEST

CORRECT ACTION
• Be sure to keep your forearms parallel to the ground

AVOID
• Keeping your elbows in

1

2

Upper Chest Stretch

The Upper Chest Stretch promotes flexibility in the chest, which is important for true upper-body strength and mobility. It works on the pectorals, anterior deltoids, and biceps.

Step 1 Begin in a standing position, with your left arm drawn straight out to the side and your palm planted against a solid surface—a wall or doorframe, for example.

Step 2 Keeping your feet planted on the floor and your left arm parallel to the ground, turn your upper body to the right, away from the wall, feeling a stretch across the chest. Hold for 10–30 seconds, then switch arms.

CORRECT ACTION
- Keep your feet and lower body still
- Keep your arm straight, at about shoulder level

AVOID
- Turning at your hips

TARGET MUSCLES

deltoideus anterior

pectoralis major

pectoralis minor

biceps brachii

CHEST, SHOULDERS, AND ARMS

Rolling Quadriceps Stretch

The Rolling Quadriceps Stretch stimulates myofascial release in the quadriceps. It is a relatively easy way of loosening any tight areas in your quad muscles and generally alleviating tension in your upper legs.

Step 1 Lie facedown, supporting your weight on your hands, with your lower body slightly rotated so that your right leg rests on a foam roller. The roller should be situated between your knee and your hip.

Step 2 Keeping both legs and feet off the floor, roll over the area between your knee and your hip. Hold for 10–30 seconds at the highest point of tension, then switch legs.

CORRECT ACTION
• Look for a controlled range of motion

AVOID
• Rolling too fast
• Overextending your lower back
• If you feel any pain, cease immediately

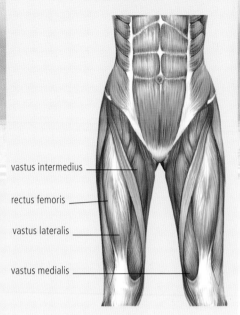

TARGET MUSCLES

vastus intermedius

rectus femoris

vastus lateralis

vastus medialis

QUADRICEPS

Rolling Hamstring Stretch

Hamstrings are susceptible to becoming tight, which can lead to tearing. It is therefore essential that they are stretched before and after any kind of workout. This routine is ideal for releasing tension in the hamstrings.

Step 1 Begin in a seated position, with a foam roller placed underneath your upper legs, and your hands either to the side or behind you for support. Bend your left leg and shift your weight onto the right leg.

Step 2 Keeping your right foot off the floor, begin rolling over the belly of the muscle. Hold for 10–30 seconds at the highest point of tension, then switch legs.

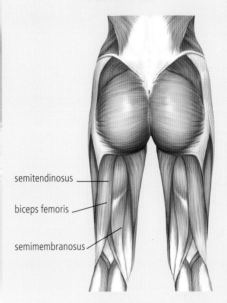

TARGET MUSCLES

semitendinosus

biceps femoris

semimembranosus

HAMSTRINGS

CORRECT ACTION
- Keep your back straight

AVOID
- Rolling too fast

Leg and Hip Exercises

The legs include the largest muscles in the human body and are key to standing, sitting, and all types of motion. Leg and hip training results not only in raw, full-body strength, but also in a muscular symmetry of the body and improved cardiovascular performance. Those who choose not to train legs, or who claim that cardiovascular exercise alone is sufficient, miss out on the truly spectacular benefits of targeting these muscles regularly in the gym.

Seated Leg Extension

The Seated Leg Extension is a great strengthening exercise for the quadriceps. By keeping the tension on the intended muscles throughout the movement, this exercise will effectively work the quadriceps through a full range of motion.

Step 1 Begin seated in a leg-extension machine with your feet under the pads and your body firmly locked in place.

Step 2 Exhale as you bend your legs upward as far as they can go so they are fully contracted.

Step 3 Inhale as you slowly lower the legs back down to the starting position. Continue to complete 12 to 15 repetitions.

CORRECT ACTION
- Look for a controlled range of motion
- Aim for full contraction and extension

AVOID
- Speedy repetitions
- Short range of motion
- Leaning your upper body too far forward

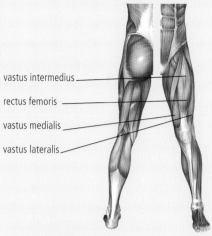

TARGET MUSCLES

vastus intermedius
rectus femoris
vastus medialis
vastus lateralis

REAR   FRONT

QUADRICEPS

Lying Leg Curls

This exercise is one of the most effective leg-strengthening exercises. Working through an explosive full range of motion, the Lying Leg Curl is to the legs what the Barbell Curl is to the arms.

Step 1 Begin by lying facedown on a leg-curl machine with your lower legs under the rollers.

Step 2 Exhale as you bend your legs back at the knee until fully contracted at the top near the glute muscles.

Step 3 Inhale as you slowly lower your legs back down to lengthen the muscle. Continue to complete 10 to 12 repetitions.

CORRECT ACTION
- Look for a controlled range of motion
- Aim for full contraction and extension

AVOID
- Speedy repetitions
- Short range of motion
- Hyperextending your lower back

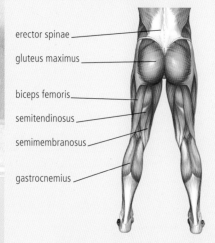

TARGET MUSCLES

erector spinae
gluteus maximus
biceps femoris
semitendinosus
semimembranosus
gastrocnemius

GLUTES AND HAMSTRINGS

Kettlebell Figure-Eight

The Kettlebell Figure-Eight is a strength builder, primarily of the trunk and hips. Strength, coordination, timing, and accuracy are required to perform this exercise correctly. The routine is slow-paced and is performed for longer amounts of time than most exercises— in doing so it helps to develop "slow strength" and muscular endurance rather than explosive power or speed.

Step 1 Begin with a kettlebell in hand, legs in a wide stance with your glutes out, bent over and with a flat back.

Step 2 Start by passing the kettlebell from one hand to another between your legs.

Step 3 Reach from behind the leg with the receiving hand and switch the kettlebell.

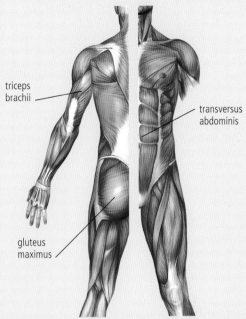

TARGET MUSCLES

triceps brachii

transversus abdominis

gluteus maximus

REAR   FRONT

TRUNK AND HIPS

Step 4 Make 20 passes between the hands.

Step 5 After completing 20 passes, switch directions. Instead of switching hands, swing the kettlebell back out with the same hand and back in front of the same leg it just circled around.

Step 6 Perform another 20 passes.

CORRECT ACTION
• Look for slow and controlled repetitions
• Keep your back flat throughout the movement
• Move your hips side to side during the movement

AVOID
• Excessive speed
• Bouncy repetitions
• Shallow or incomplete passes

3

Standing One-Legged Curls

Standing One-Legged Curls isolate the hamstrings and are designed to effectively finish off training of the hamstrings during your workout.

Step 1 Begin by standing up straight with your feet together and your arms by your sides.

Step 2 Exhale as you bend one leg back and upward in a curling motion until fully contracted at the top, near the glute muscles.

Step 3 Inhale as you lower your leg back down slowly to lengthen the muscle. Continue to complete 12 to 15 repetitions per leg.

TARGET MUSCLES

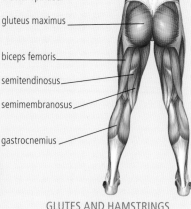

erector spinae

gluteus maximus

biceps femoris

semitendinosus

semimembranosus

gastrocnemius

GLUTES AND HAMSTRINGS

CORRECT ACTION
- Look for a controlled range of motion
- Look for peak contraction
- Aim at full extension

AVOID
- Speedy repetitions
- Short range of motion
- Leaning your upper body backward

Kettlebell Pass

The Kettlebell Pass is a lunge variation with a shortened range of motion. It is a strength builder for many parts of the body, but also develops the coordination required for many sports. Timing plays a critical factor in its proper execution.

Step 1 Start by holding a kettlebell in one hand, with your back straight and your legs bent at the knees.

Step 2 Stand up straight and, at the top of the motion, pass the kettlebell to your other hand.

Step 3 Return to your original position with your knees bent. Continue to complete 10 repetitions, alternating the hand that begins the exercise holding the kettlebell.

TARGET MUSCLES

deltoideus anterior

transversus abdominis

biceps femoris

semitendinosus

semimembranosus

REAR   FRONT

HAMSTRINGS

CORRECT ACTION
- Look for proper timing and tempo during repetitions
- Keep your back flat throughout the movement
- Strive for a proper range of motion

AVOID
- Excessive speed
- Bouncy repetitions
- Shallow or incomplete passes

Barbell Squats

The iconic Barbell Squat is one of the most effective strengthening exercises you can take on. It is fantastic for strengthening the lower body and the core, and has a positive effect on your metabolism.

Step 1 Begin by standing in front of a barbell (at eye level) in a power rack and duck beneath it so that the barbell is resting on the rear of your shoulders. Place your feet shoulder-width apart.

Step 2 Walk the barbell out of the rack and inhale as you bend at the knees. Keep your back flat and lower yourself toward the ground until your thighs are parallel to the floor.

Step 3 Exhale as you push through your heels to stand erect. Complete 10 to 12 repetitions.

CORRECT ACTION
- Squat until your thighs are parallel to the ground
- Look for a slow and controlled lowering of the weight
- Push through your heels to drive the movement

AVOID
- Hyperextending your knees past your thighs
- A rounded back
- A shortened range of motion

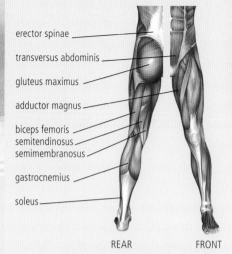

TARGET MUSCLES

erector spinae
transversus abdominis
gluteus maximus
adductor magnus
biceps femoris
semitendinosus
semimembranosus
gastrocnemius
soleus

REAR   FRONT

GLUTES AND HAMSTRINGS

Swiss Ball Squats

Swiss Ball Squats are an effective alternative to conventional squats. While providing many of the same benefits as traditional squats, they also help to alleviate pressure on the lower back.

Step 1 Begin by standing in front of a wall with a Swiss ball in your hands. Place your feet shoulder-width apart. Lean back so the wall is touching the middle of your back.

Step 2 Inhale as you bend at the knees. Keep your back flat and lower yourself down until your thighs are parallel to the ground.

Step 3 Exhale as you push through your heels to stand erect. Continue to complete 10 to 12 repetitions.

CORRECT ACTION
• Squat until your thighs are parallel to the ground
• Look for a slow and controlled descent
• Push through your heels to drive the movement

AVOID
• Hyperextending your knees past your thighs
• Bouncy repetitions
• A shortened range of motion

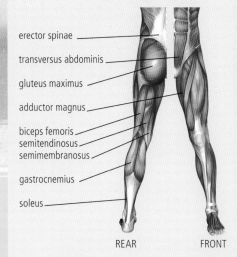

TARGET MUSCLES

erector spinae
transversus abdominis
gluteus maximus
adductor magnus
biceps femoris
semitendinosus
semimembranosus
gastrocnemius
soleus

REAR   FRONT

GLUTES AND HAMSTRINGS

Hack Squats

Hack Squats are another good alternative to traditional Barbell Squats in that they place most of the stress on the quadriceps muscles while alleviating pressure on the lower back. They also enhance the sweep of the legs.

Step 1 Unrack a barbell and hold it at arm's length with your feet shoulder-width apart. One hand should be holding the bar with your palm facing down, the other with your palm facing up.

Step 2 Inhale as you bend at the knees. Lower yourself toward the ground until your thighs are parallel to it.

Step 3 Exhale as you push through your heels to stand erect. Complete 10 to 12 repetitions.

CORRECT ACTION
- Squat until your thighs are parallel to the ground
- Look for a slow and controlled lowering of the weight
- Push through your heels to drive the movement

AVOID
- Hyperextending your knees past your thighs
- Bouncy repetitions
- A shortened range of motion

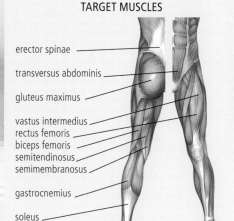

TARGET MUSCLES

erector spinae
transversus abdominis
gluteus maximus
vastus intermedius
rectus femoris
biceps femoris
semitendinosus
semimembranosus
gastrocnemius
soleus

REAR   FRONT

QUADS AND HAMSTRINGS

Band Good Morning

The Band Good Morning targets the hamstrings, glutes, and lower back. It increases power in the hamstrings, particularly the semitendinosus, biceps femoris, and semimembranosus muscles.

Step 1 Loop a band around the base of a post. Step back a short distance and place the other end of the band over your head; it should sit on the back of your neck. Hold the band in place with your hands.

Step 2 Keeping your feet shoulder-width apart, your knees slightly bent, and your back flat, lean forward at the waist until your back is nearly parallel to the ground. Drive through the hips to return to the starting position. Complete 12 to 15 repetitions.

TARGET MUSCLES

gluteus maximus

biceps femoris

semitendinosus

semimembranosus

HAMSTRINGS AND GLUTES

CORRECT ACTION
• Keep your back flat and your rear sticking out

AVOID
• Creating an excessive range of motion throughout the exercise

1

2

One-Legged Extension

The One-Legged Extension is an advanced version of the classic leg extension, which places emphasis on the core as well as the legs. An effective leg-strengthener as well as a stabilizer, this version of the extension is particularly effective for isolating the individual sections of the leg muscles.

Step 1 Begin seated on a leg-extension machine, with your back against the pad, one foot under the roller, and your knee in line with your foot. Your other foot should be on the ground.

Step 2 Raise the weight up until your leg is fully extended, then slowly return the leg back to its original position.

Step 3 Complete 10 to 12 repetitions and then switch legs.

CORRECT ACTION
• Push through the heel to drive the movement
• Raise until your leg is as straight as possible
• Keep your knee in line with your foot

AVOID
• Pushing through your toes
• Shallow repetitions
• Allowing your lower back and rear to angle up

TARGET MUSCLES

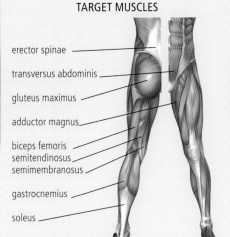

erector spinae
transversus abdominis
gluteus maximus
adductor magnus
biceps femoris
semitendinosus
semimembranosus
gastrocnemius
soleus

CORE AND HAMSTRINGS   REAR   FRONT

Power Squat

The Power Squat is an easy way of strengthening the glutes and thighs. It also improves balance; helps to stabilize the pelvis, trunk, and knees; and boosts general movement strength.

WARNING Not advisable if you have sharp knee pain, lower-back pain, or shoulder pain.

Step 1 Stand upright, holding a weighted ball in front of your torso.

Step 2 Shift your weight to your left foot and bend your right knee, lifting your right foot toward your buttocks. Bend your elbows and draw the ball toward the outside of your right ear.

Step 3 Maintaining a neutral spine, bend at your hips and knee. Lower your torso toward your left side, bringing the ball toward your right ankle.

Step 4 Press into your left leg and straighten your knee and torso, returning to the starting position. Repeat 15 times for two sets on each leg.

CORRECT ACTION
- Ensure the ball creates an arc in the air
- Keep your hips and knees aligned throughout the movement
- Try to keep your shoulders and neck relaxed through the exercise

AVOID
- Allowing your knee to extend beyond your toes as you bend and rotate
- Moving your foot from its starting position
- Flexing your spine

TARGET MUSCLES

erector spinae

gluteus maximus

vastus intermedius

rectus femoris

tibialis anterior

GLUTES AND THIGHS   REAR   FRONT

Lateral Low Lunge

The Lateral Low Lunge concentrates on the gluteal and thigh muscles. It is excellent for strengthening the pelvic, trunk, and knee stabilizers.

WARNING Not advisable if you have sharp knee pain, back pain, or if you have trouble bearing weight on one leg.

Step 1 Stand upright with your hips and arms outstretched in front of you, parallel to the floor.

Step 2 Step out to the left. Squat down on your right leg, bending at your hips, while maintaining a neutral spine. Begin to extend your left leg, keeping both feet flat on the floor.

Step 3 Bend your right knee until your thigh is parallel to the floor, and your left leg is fully extended.

Step 4 Keeping your arms parallel to the ground, squeeze your buttocks and press off your right leg to return to the starting position, and repeat. Repeat the sequence 10 times on each side.

CORRECT ACTION
- Keep your spine neutral as you bend your hips
- Try to keep your shoulders and neck relaxed
- Your knee should align with the toe of your bent leg

AVOID
- Craning your neck as you perform the movement
- Lifting your feet off the floor
- Arching or extending your back

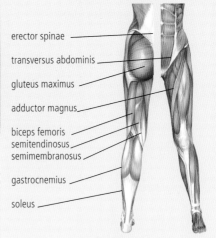

TARGET MUSCLES

erector spinae
transversus abdominis
gluteus maximus
adductor magnus
biceps femoris
semitendinosus
semimembranosus
gastrocnemius
soleus

REAR   FRONT

GLUTES AND THIGHS

Air Squats

Air Squats are beneficial for the quadriceps, hamstrings, glutes, and core. They serve to increase power and mass in the thighs. As a variation, you can place a Swiss ball against a wall and lean your lower back into it; to increase the difficulty level, bring your feet closer together as this increases the effort required to complete the squat.

Step 1 Stand tall, with your feet shoulder-width apart, your toes pointed slightly outward, and your arms extended in front of you.

Step 2 Inhale as you bend your knees, while keeping your back straight. Lower yourself toward the floor until your thighs are parallel to it.

Step 3 Exhale as you push through your heels to stand erect. Perform 12 to 15 repetitions.

CORRECT ACTION
- Squat deep, and be sure to keep your thighs parallel to the floor

AVOID
- Hyperextending your knees past your toes while squatting

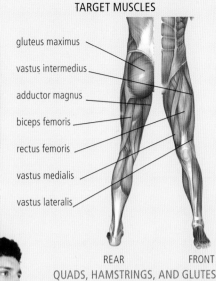

TARGET MUSCLES

gluteus maximus
vastus intermedius
adductor magnus
biceps femoris
rectus femoris
vastus medialis
vastus lateralis

REAR   FRONT
QUADS, HAMSTRINGS, AND GLUTES

Barbell Squat Snatch

The Barbell Squat Snatch is aimed at boosting the deltoids and glutes, while also working the upper back, core, and hamstrings. It is especially beneficial for increasing power and mass in the shoulders and thighs. As an easier variation, do the exercise using very light dumbbells or just your own body weight.

Step 1 Begin by standing with your feet shoulder-width apart in front of a barbell. Squat down and grab the barbell with a wide overhand grip. Make sure your knees are close to the bar.

Step 2 As you return to a standing position, flip the barbell directly up above your chest.

Step 3 Stand fully erect while pressing the barbell overhead to complete the movement.

Step 4 Lower the barbell carefully to your chest and then down to the ground. Perform 6 to 8 repetitions.

1

2

CORRECT ACTION
• Use your legs to help with the movement

AVOID
• Overarching your back

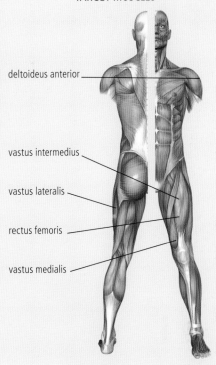

TARGET MUSCLES

deltoideus anterior

vastus intermedius

vastus lateralis

rectus femoris

vastus medialis

REAR   FRONT

SHOULDERS AND GLUTES

3

MODIFICATION

Easier: Execute the exercise using very light dumbbells or just your own body weight.

Box Jumps

Box Jumps target the quadriceps, hamstrings, and glutes. They generate explosive power in your lower body. An easier option is to use a lower platform for the exercise, while a higher platform will make it more demanding.

Step 1 Stand in front of a stable box or platform.

Step 2 Drop down into a quarter-squat in preparation for your jump.

Step 3 Push through your heels, swing your arms, and spring up onto the box.

Step 4 Land softly on your heels, then step down. Perform 15 repetitions.

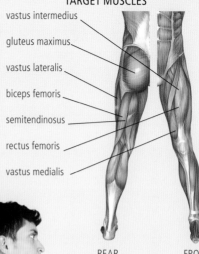

TARGET MUSCLES

vastus intermedius

gluteus maximus

vastus lateralis

biceps femoris

semitendinosus

rectus femoris

vastus medialis

REAR   FRONT

QUADS, HAMSTRINGS, AND GLUTES

CORRECT ACTION
• Be sure to keep a tight core throughout the movement

AVOID
• Landing excessively hard

Burpees

Burpees are aimed at the glutes, quadriceps, hamstrings, and calves. They serve to increase both muscular strength and endurance. You can make it easier by jumping at a very low height, while adding a push-up to the routine will add an extra level of difficulty.

TARGET MUSCLES

gluteus maximus
vastus intermedius
vastus lateralis
biceps femoris
semitendinosus
rectus femoris
vastus medialis
gastrocnemius

REAR   FRONT

GLUTES, QUADS, HAMSTRINGS, AND CALVES

Step 1 Begin in a squat position, with your hands firmly planted on the floor, shoulder-width apart.

Step 2 Kick your feet back and straighten your legs into a push-up position.

Step 3 Quickly return to the squat position.

Step 4 Leap vertically from the squat position as high as possible, raising your arms as you jump. Complete 15 repetitions.

CORRECT ACTION
• Be sure to keep a tight core throughout the movement

AVOID
• Landing excessively hard

Cone Jumps

Cone Jumps benefit the quadriceps, hamstrings, glutes, and calves. They help you practice lateral movement at speed. An easier variation is to complete a set of jumps to one side, and then switch. On the other hand, you can make the routine more difficult by adding a series of cones.

Step 1 Stand to the right of a cone. Jump off both feet to your left to clear the cone, landing on your left foot only.

Step 2 Put your right foot down, and leap off both feet to clear the cone again. Be sure to land on your right foot this time. Only the foot that will be farthest away from the cone should make contact with the ground. Perform 15 repetitions per side.

CORRECT ACTION
• Be sure to keep a tight core throughout the movement

AVOID
• Allowing your knees to protrude past your toes when landing

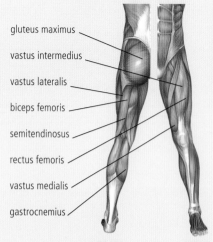

TARGET MUSCLES

gluteus maximus
vastus intermedius
vastus lateralis
biceps femoris
semitendinosus
rectus femoris
vastus medialis
gastrocnemius

REAR   FRONT

QUADS, HAMSTRINGS, GLUTES, AND CALVES

Crossover Step-Up

The Crossover Step-Up targets the quadriceps, hamstrings, and glutes. It is especially good for increasing power and explosiveness in the thighs. You could use a stick or broom for support, or you can make it more demanding by holding a pair of dumbbells for increased resistance.

Step 1 Stand to the right of a bench.

Step 2 Cross your right leg in front of your left and step up onto the bench. Push through the stabilized right heel on the bench to raise yourself up.

Step 3 Bring the left leg up onto the bench, then perform the motion in reverse to step down. Repeat 15 times per leg before switching to the other side.

CORRECT ACTION
- Maintain an erect posture throughout the movement

AVOID
- Hyperextending your knee past your toes

TARGET MUSCLES

- gluteus maximus
- vastus intermedius
- vastus lateralis
- biceps femoris
- semitendinosus
- rectus femoris
- vastus medialis

QUADS, HAMSTRINGS, AND GLUTES   REAR   FRONT

Depth Jumps

Depth Jumps benefit the quadriceps, hamstrings, glutes, and calves. They improve your speed, power, and general athleticism. As a variation, you can use your arms to increase speed or even make the routine more challenging by using higher platforms.

Step 1 Place two platforms about 3 feet apart from each other. Stand on top of the first platform.

Step 2 Jump off the platform; be sure to land in front of the next one on the balls of your feet.

Step 3 As soon as your feet hit the ground, spring up onto the other platform.

Step 4 Immediately after landing on the second platform, turn around and start again. Repeat 15 times.

CORRECT ACTION
• Be sure to maintain an erect posture throughout the movement

AVOID
• Landing on your toes or heels

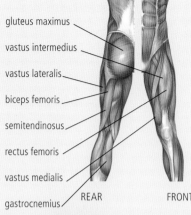

TARGET MUSCLES

gluteus maximus

vastus intermedius

vastus lateralis

biceps femoris

semitendinosus

rectus femoris

vastus medialis

gastrocnemius

REAR   FRONT

QUADS, HAMSTRINGS, GLUTES, AND CALVES

Goblet Squat

The Goblet Squat targets the quadriceps, calves, glutes, and hamstrings. It is especially good for building strength in the quadriceps. Taking a wider stance will reduce the range of motion and make the exercise less demanding, while a closer stance will increase the range and make it more difficult.

Step 1 While in a standing position, hold a kettlebell with both hands close to your chest. Your legs should be a little more than shoulder-width apart, with your toes pointing slightly outward.

Step 2 Squat down until your thighs are parallel to the floor, bringing your elbows to your thighs.

Step 3 Keep your back flat as you push through your heels back to the standing position. Complete 8 to 10 repetitions.

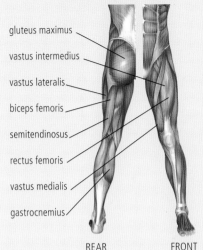

TARGET MUSCLES

gluteus maximus
vastus intermedius
vastus lateralis
biceps femoris
semitendinosus
rectus femoris
vastus medialis
gastrocnemius

REAR   FRONT

QUADS, HAMSTRINGS, GLUTES, AND CALVES

CORRECT ACTION
- Always employ a full range of motion

AVOID
- Hyperextending your knees past your toes

Hip Extension with Band

The Hip Extension with Band focuses on your glutes and hamstrings. In particular, it builds strength in the three muscles that make up the glutes—the gluteus minimus, medius, and maximus.

Step 1 Loop one end of a band to the lower part of a post, and wrap the other end around your right ankle or foot.

Step 2 Stand facing the post, holding a stable surface for support.

Step 3 Maintaining an upright posture, extend your right leg as far back as you are able while also keeping it as straight as possible. Complete 10 to 12 repetitions, then switch legs.

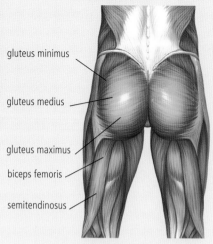

TARGET MUSCLES

gluteus minimus

gluteus medius

gluteus maximus

biceps femoris

semitendinosus

GLUTES AND HAMSTRINGS

CORRECT ACTION
• Maintain an upright posture throughout the movement

AVOID
• An excessive kicking motion

Lateral Bounding

Lateral Bounding targets several areas, including the quadriceps, hamstrings, glutes, and calves. Its principal aim is to help you practice lateral movement at speed. Try completing a set of jumps to one side, and then switching. Alternatively, add an extra level of difficulty by performing the routine while holding a medicine ball.

Step 1 Start in a quarter-squat position, then bound off your right foot as far and high as possible to your left.

Step 2 Be sure to land on your left foot.

Step 3 Next, bound as far and as high as possible back to your right off your left foot. Perform 15 repetitions per side.

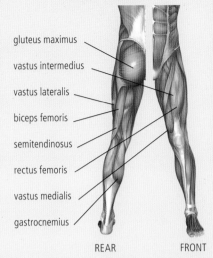

TARGET MUSCLES

gluteus maximus

vastus intermedius

vastus lateralis

biceps femoris

semitendinosus

rectus femoris

vastus medialis

gastrocnemius

REAR   FRONT

QUADS, HAMSTRINGS, GLUTES, AND CALVES

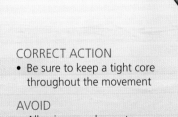

CORRECT ACTION
• Be sure to keep a tight core throughout the movement

AVOID
• Allowing your knees to protrude past your toes

2

3

Mountain Climber

The Mountain Climber is a stability exercise that also tests and extends the endurance and the activation of many muscles working together to execute the movement. This is a taxing and repetitious exercise that, quite simply, works.

WARNING Not advisable if you have wrist pain, shoulder issues, or lower-back pain.

Step 1 Begin in a completed push-up position with your body maintained in a straight line.

Step 2 Raise one leg and bring your knee as close to your chest as you can, then return to the starting position.

Step 3 Repeat with the other leg, alternating both for 30 seconds to 2 minutes.

CORRECT ACTION
• Keep a tight core throughout the movement
• Breathe throughout the exercise
• Be light on your toes

AVOID
• Your toes hitting the ground excessively hard
• Holding your breath
• Excessively bridging your back

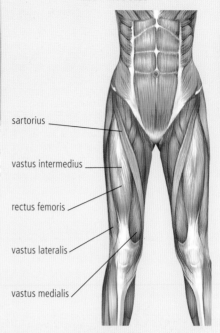

TARGET MUSCLES

sartorius

vastus intermedius

rectus femoris

vastus lateralis

vastus medialis

QUADRICEPS

One-Arm Kettlebell Clean

The One-Arm Kettlebell Clean works mainly on the hamstrings and glutes, as well as the lower back, shoulders, and trapezius. It is great for building strength in the hamstrings. You can widen or reduce your stance to respectively reduce or increase your range of motion.

Step 1 Take a standing position, with your feet shoulder-width apart and knees slightly bent, holding a kettlebell in one hand.

Step 2 Bend down as you push your rear out behind you, with your eyes looking straight ahead.

Step 3 Clean the kettlebell to your shoulder by rotating the wrist and extending through the legs and hips. Return to the starting position. Complete 8 to 10 repetitions per arm.

CORRECT ACTION
- Work cohesively with your opposing muscles

AVOID
- Using excessive momentum when cleaning the kettlebell to your shoulder

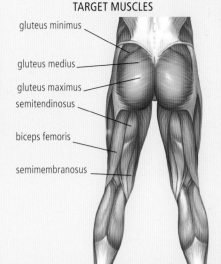

TARGET MUSCLES

gluteus minimus

gluteus medius

gluteus maximus

semitendinosus

biceps femoris

semimembranosus

HAMSTRINGS AND GLUTES

Reverse Lunge

The Reverse Lunge targets the quadriceps, glutes, and hamstrings. Its main benefit is that it strengthens the quadriceps and glutes. Use a broom or stick for support or, as a further modification of the routine, hold a pair of dumbbells for increased resistance.

Step 1 Stand with your hands on your hips and your feet shoulder-width apart.

Step 2 Take a big step backwards, bending your knees as you do so.

Step 3 When the front thigh is roughly parallel to the ground, push through your front heel to return to the starting position. Perform 15 repetitions per leg.

TARGET MUSCLES

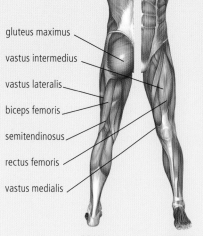

- gluteus maximus
- vastus intermedius
- vastus lateralis
- biceps femoris
- semitendinosus
- rectus femoris
- vastus medialis

REAR   FRONT

QUADS, GLUTES, AND HAMSTRINGS

CORRECT ACTION
- Maintain an erect posture throughout the movement

AVOID
- Hyperextending your knee past your toes when lunging

MODIFICATION

More difficult: Use a pair of dumbbells.

Standing Calf Raise

The diamond-shaped gastrocnemius muscles—known as the calves—are the often-stubborn muscles that require heavy weights and many repetitions to work them effectively, as they are used constantly when walking. Although the shape and insertion point of this muscle is largely a result of genetics, even the most underdeveloped calves can be improved through the use of this standing version of the calf raise. This routine can be carried out in a gym or at home.

Step 1 Begin by standing with a weight barbell across your shoulders (or by ducking under the shoulder pads on a standing calf-raise machine).

Step 2 Rise up on your toes, contracting the calf muscles at the top. Then lower back down for 12 to 15 repetitions.

CORRECT ACTION
- Maintain a full range of motion
- Contract the muscles at the top of the movement
- Keep your toes pointed straight

AVOID
- Partial repetitions
- Bouncy and speedy repetitions
- Changing the position of your feet during the movement

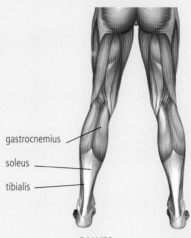

TARGET MUSCLES

gastrocnemius

soleus

tibialis

CALVES

Seated Calf Raise

The seated version of the Calf Raise is similar to the standing version. However, by sitting down there is less stress on the lower back and more tension on the calf muscle throughout the range of motion. This explosive exercise enables you to build up calf strength and size.

Step 1 Begin seated at a calf-raise machine with your thighs under the roller.

Step 2 As you rise up on your toes, contract the calf muscles at the top, then lower back down for a full stretch of 12 to 15 repetitions.

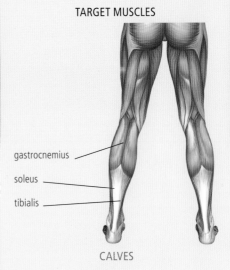

TARGET MUSCLES

gastrocnemius

soleus

tibialis

CALVES

CORRECT ACTION
- Maintain a full range of motion
- Contract the muscles at the top of the movement
- Keep your toes pointed straight on

AVOID
- Partial repetitions
- Bouncy and speedy repetitions
- Changing the position of your feet during the movement

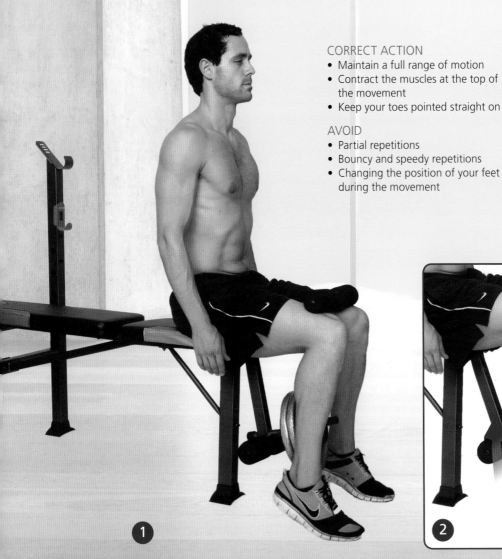

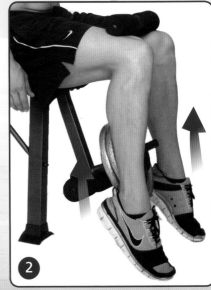

Star Jumps

Star Jumps are beneficial for the quadriceps, hamstrings, glutes, and calves. They are a relatively simple way of developing explosive power in your lower body. You can vary the routine's difficulty level by modifying the height at which you jump; quite simply, the higher you leap, the more demanding it will be.

Step 1 Start by crouching down in a half-squat position, with your arms slightly bent in front of you and your hands crossed over each other.

Step 2 Push off your heels and leap straight up, extending your legs to the side and raising your arms as you do so. Land softly on your heels, then return to the starting position. Perform 15 repetitions.

CORRECT ACTION
• Be sure to keep a tight core throughout the movement

AVOID
• Landing excessively hard

TARGET MUSCLES

gluteus maximus
vastus intermedius
vastus lateralis
biceps femoris
semitendinosus
rectus femoris
vastus medialis
gastrocnemius

REAR   FRONT

QUADS, HAMSTRINGS, GLUTES, AND CALVES

1

2

Core Exercises

The core comprises a range of muscles from the neck down to the hips, including the abdominals, erector spinae, the obliques, multifidus, and transversus abdominis. Training the core is important for several reasons, not least because it stabilizes your spine to provide a solid base from which you can develop other areas of your body. Core strength is also great for general athletic performance and reduces the chance of injuring your back during training.

Sit-Up

The Sit-Up is to the abdominals what the Bench Press is to the pectorals: a highly effective exercise. The iconic Sit-Up is widely used on a daily basis and for good reason—it is the perfect exercise for the rectus abdominis. It is similar to the crunch, but Sit-Ups have a fuller range of motion and condition additional muscles.

Step 1 Begin by lying on your back with your legs bent and your hands behind your head.

Step 2 Start by pushing through your heels for support and raising your trunk off the ground, contracting your abdominals while lifting up toward your knees.

Step 3 Lower and repeat for 20 repetitions.

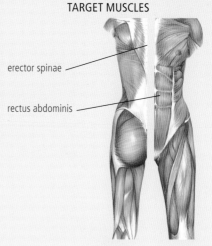

TARGET MUSCLES

erector spinae

rectus abdominis

REAR   FRONT
ABDOMINALS

CORRECT ACTION
• Lead from your belly button
• A controlled lowering
• A precise range of motion

AVOID
• Overusing your neck
• Stressing your lower back
• Swinging upward wildly

Advanced Kettlebell Windmill

The Advanced Kettlebell Windmill is aimed at the abdominals, glutes, hamstrings, and shoulders. Its main benefit is to increase strength in the abdominals. You can also execute the exercise without a kettlebell.

Step 1 With your right arm by your side and your feet shoulder-width apart, stand with a kettlebell in your left hand, raised overhead.

Step 2 Push your left hip out to the left and slightly bend your knees while lowering your torso to the right as far as possible. Pause, then return to the starting position. Complete 8 to 10 repetitions per side.

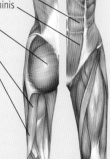

TARGET MUSCLES

deltoideus anterior

rectus abdominis

transversus abdominis

gluteus maximus

biceps femoris
semitendinosus

REAR   FRONT
ABDOMINALS, GLUTES,
HAMSTRINGS, AND SHOULDERS

CORRECT ACTION
• Keep your back flat throughout the movement

AVOID
• Bouncing excessively and using momentum

Bent-Knee Sit-Up

This simple routine strengthens the hip flexors, rectus abdominis, and obliques. Add an extra degree of difficulty by carrying out the routine with one leg raised off the floor.

Step 1 Lie on your back with your legs bent so that your feet are tucked as close to your buttocks as possible. Either put your hands on your head or cross your arms over your chest.

Step 2 Flex your trunk toward your thighs until your back is off the floor, then lower yourself back down. Repeat 25 times.

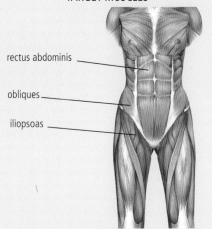

TARGET MUSCLES

rectus abdominis

obliques

iliopsoas

HIP FLEXORS, ABDOMINALS, AND OBLIQUES

CORRECT ACTION
- Be sure to engage your core, not your neck

AVOID
- Rounding your back

Farmer's Walk

The Farmer's Walk helps develop grip strength in your forearms, as well as boosting core stability. It works on the rectus abdominis, erector spinae, forearms, and biceps. You can vary the challenge by carrying a lighter or heavier weight.

Step 1 Begin in a standing position, feet shoulder-width apart, holding a pair of kettlebells or dumbbells by your side.

Step 2 Walk rapidly for a predetermined distance or time (for example, the length of the gym or 20 seconds). Lower the weights, rest, and repeat three times.

CORRECT ACTION
- Keep a tight core throughout the movement

AVOID
- Holding excessive weights

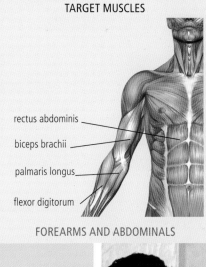

TARGET MUSCLES

rectus abdominis

biceps brachii

palmaris longus

flexor digitorum

FOREARMS AND ABDOMINALS

Kneeling Cable Crunch

The Kneeling Cable Crunch takes the standard crunch and adds resistance to it, thereby making this a very effective core-strengthening exercise suitable for all levels.

WARNING Avoid this exercise if you have lower-back pain.

Step 1 Begin on your knees, with a rope held around your neck, facing away from a weight stack, set to a moderate resistance.

Step 2 Start by bending forward at the waist, keeping your neck tucked, and crunch downward, until your elbows are resting on your thighs.

Step 3 Contract the abdominals, then return to the starting position, and repeat for 30 repetitions.

CORRECT ACTION
- Maintain a full range of motion
- Contract the muscles together at the bottom of the movement
- A straightened torso at the top

AVOID
- Excessive speed
- A shortened range of motion
- Using too much neck at the expense of your abdominals

TARGET MUSCLES

rectus abdominis

obliques

erector spinae

hip flexors

REAR   FRONT

ABDOMINALS AND OBLIQUES

1

2

Medicine Ball Pike-Up

The Medicine Ball Pike-Up is aimed at the core, glutes, hamstrings, and calves. The routine is especially good for building strength and stability in the core. You can perform the exercise without a medicine ball or make it more of a challenge by raising one leg off the ball.

Step 1 Begin in a standard push-up position, with your hands shoulder-width apart and your toes planted on a medicine ball.

Step 2 Raise your hips to the ceiling, rolling the medicine ball toward your hands as you do so.

Step 3 Reverse the movement, lowering yourself back down to the starting position. Complete 15 repetitions.

CORRECT ACTION
• Keep your legs locked throughout the movement

AVOID
• Lowering your torso farther than parallel to the floor

TARGET MUSCLES

rectus abdominis

transversus abdominis

multifidus spinae

obliques

REAR   FRONT

ABDOMINALS AND OBLIQUES

MODIFICATION

Easier: Perform the exercise without a medicine ball.

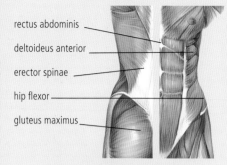

rectus abdominis

deltoideus anterior

erector spinae

hip flexor

gluteus maximus

ABDOMINALS AND SHOULDERS

Medicine Ball Slam

The Medicine Ball Slam is an effective means for engaging and readying the frontal core. It is a power movement that involves explosiveness as well as targeting. A noisy exercise, it is best performed on a solid floor.

Step 1 Begin by holding a medicine ball behind your head with your elbows bent.

Step 2 Swing the ball over your head and throw it straight down with force, squatting as you do so.

Step 3 Catch the ball in the squat position. Stand up and repeat for 20 repetitions.

CORRECT ACTION
- Be sure to keep your torso straight throughout the movement
- Keep a tight core throughout
- Keep your arms bent
- Keep your eyes on the ball

AVOID
- Excessively rounding your back

1

2

Medicine Ball Woodchopper

Another straightforward routine using a medicine ball, the Medicine Ball Woodchopper targets the obliques, rectus abdominis, and erectors. Its principal benefit is to strengthen the obliques.

Step 1 Stand upright, with your feet shoulder-width apart, holding a medicine ball with both hands to the right side of your head.

Step 2 Twist your core toward the left while lowering the medicine ball to the outside of your left leg, then return to the starting position. Repeat 20 times, then switch to the other side.

CORRECT ACTION
- Perform the positive portion of the exercise (swinging) aggressively and the negative portion (the wind-up) in a slow, controlled fashion, all the while keeping your core contracted and tight

AVOID
- Twisting too violently from side to side, since this can throw out your back

TARGET MUSCLES

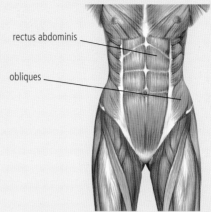

rectus abdominis

obliques

OBLIQUES

Plank

The Plank is a conditioning routine that focuses on the rectus abdominis, erector spinae, and oblique muscles. It is excellent for strengthening the entire core. For a greater challenge, lift one foot off the floor while carrying out the exercise.

Step 1 Position yourself on all fours.

Step 2 Plant your forearms on the floor parallel to one another, then raise your knees off the floor and lengthen your legs until they are in line with your arms.

Step 3 Hold this plank position for 30 seconds (building up to 2 minutes).

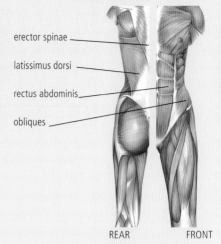

TARGET MUSCLES

erector spinae

latissimus dorsi

rectus abdominis

obliques

REAR   FRONT

ABDOMINALS AND OBLIQUES

CORRECT ACTION
• Keep your abdominal muscles tight and your body in a straight line

AVOID
• Bridging too high, since this can take stress off working muscles

Pullover Pass

The Pullover Pass is a particularly effective way of developing explosive strength in the abdominals. As well as the rectus abdominis, the routine also works on the erector spinae.

Step 1 Lie on your back, with your knees bent and your feet flat on the floor. Hold a medicine ball behind your head at arm's length.

Step 2 Quickly sit up, and pass the ball to a partner while contracting your abdominals.

Step 3 Receive the ball back, and gently return to the starting position. Complete 25 repetitions.

CORRECT ACTION
• Keep a tight core throughout the movement

AVOID
• Putting too much stress on your neck

TARGET MUSCLES

erector spinae

latissimus dorsi

rectus abdominis

REAR   FRONT

ABDOMINALS

Seated Russian Twist

The Seated Russian Twist uses a Swiss ball to develop the rectus abdominis, obliques, and erector spinae. It strengthens the major muscles of the core.

Step 1 Sit on the floor with your legs bent, knees slightly apart, holding a Swiss ball in front of you at arm's length. Lean back slightly to activate the core, keeping a flat back.

Step 2 Rotate your torso to the left as far as you can comfortably go.

Step 3 Smoothly return to the center, then continue the rotation as far to the right as possible, before returning to the center again. This is one rotation; complete 20 full rotations.

CORRECT ACTION
• Twist in a controlled motion

AVOID
• Rounding your back
• Twisting too fast

TARGET MUSCLES

teres major

erector spinae

rectus abdominis

obliques

REAR   FRONT

CORE

Side Plank

Aimed at the lower abdominals, erector spinae, and deltoids, the Side Plank is a straightforward exercise that strengthens the abdominals, lower back, and shoulders.

Step 1 Lie on your right side with your legs extended, one on top of the other. Your right arm should be bent at a 90-degree angle, with your fingers facing forward. Rest your left arm along your left hip.

Step 2 Pushing through your right forearm, raise your hips off the ground until your body is in a straight line. Hold this position for 30 seconds (working up to 60 seconds), then switch to your left side and repeat.

CORRECT ACTION
- Push evenly from both your forearm and hips

AVOID
- Placing too much strain on your shoulders

TARGET MUSCLES

deltoideus anterior

erector spinae

rectus abdominis

transversus abdominis

obliques

REAR   FRONT

CORE

MODIFICATIONS

Easier: Use your resting arm as an anchor, assisting with the lift.

More difficult: Open your legs slightly while in hold (seen here).

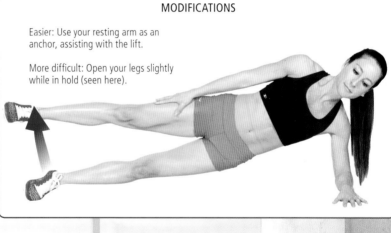

Skier

The Skier targets the hips and core, increasing stability in both. An easier variation of the routine is to rotate to one side only.

Step 1 Begin in a push-up position, with your legs resting on a Swiss ball.

Step 2 While maintaining your core position, rotate your trunk quickly to the left so that your legs are stacked on top of each other.

Step 3 Return to the starting position, and perform the same movement to the right. Complete 15 full rotations.

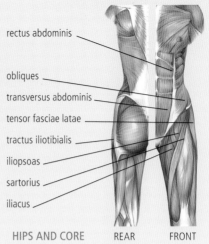

TARGET MUSCLES

rectus abdominis

obliques

transversus abdominis

tensor fasciae latae

tractus iliotibialis

iliopsoas

sartorius

iliacus

HIPS AND CORE   REAR   FRONT

CORRECT ACTION
• Keep a tight core throughout the movement

AVOID
• Excessive speed

Swiss Ball Hip Crossover

The Swiss Ball Hip Crossover helps strengthen and tone the abs, and improves core stabilization. All floor exercises are best performed on a yoga or exercise mat.

WARNING Those with lower-back problems should avoid this exercise.

Step 1 Lie on your back, with your arms extended out to your sides. Place your legs on a Swiss ball, with your glutes close to it.

Step 2 Brace your abdominal muscles, and lower your legs to one side, as close to the floor as you can without raising your shoulders off the floor.

Step 3 Return to the starting position, and then switch to the other side. Work up to completing 20 repetitions in each direction.

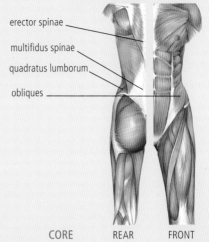

TARGET MUSCLES

erector spinae

multifidus spinae

quadratus lumborum

obliques

CORE   REAR   FRONT

CORRECT ACTION
• Keep the movement as smooth as possible

AVOID
• Swinging your hips excessively

Swiss Ball Exchange

This conditioning exercise strengthens the hip flexors and rectus abdominis, while also benefiting the erector muscles. To make the routine more challenging, you can use a medicine ball instead of a Swiss ball.

Step 1 Lie on your back, with a Swiss ball on the floor just above your head. Reach back with your arms to take hold of the ball.

Step 2 With the ball in hand, raise both your upper body and your thighs, moving them toward each other.

Step 3 Place the Swiss ball between your legs, then lower all your limbs back to the floor, bringing your arms beside your head.

Step 4 Repeat the movement, this time passing the Swiss ball from your legs to your hands. Complete 15 exchanges.

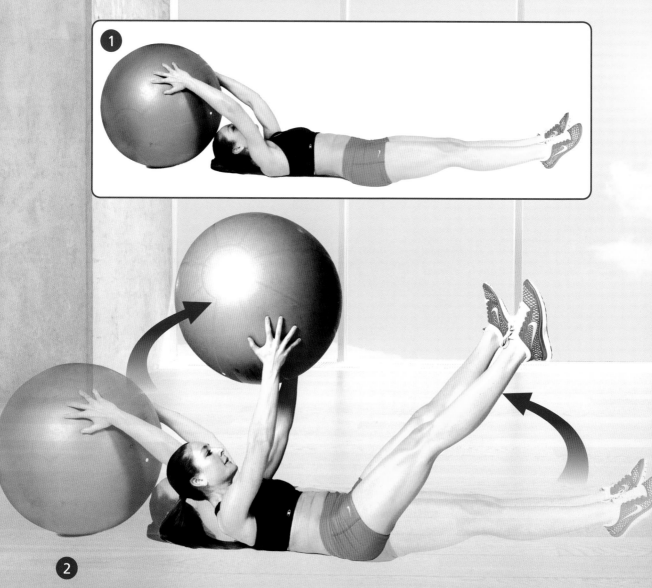

CORRECT ACTION
• Complete a full range of motion

AVOID
• Kicking up with your legs

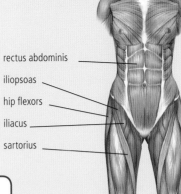

rectus abdominis
iliopsoas
hip flexors
iliacus
sartorius

HIP FLEXORS AND ABDOMINALS

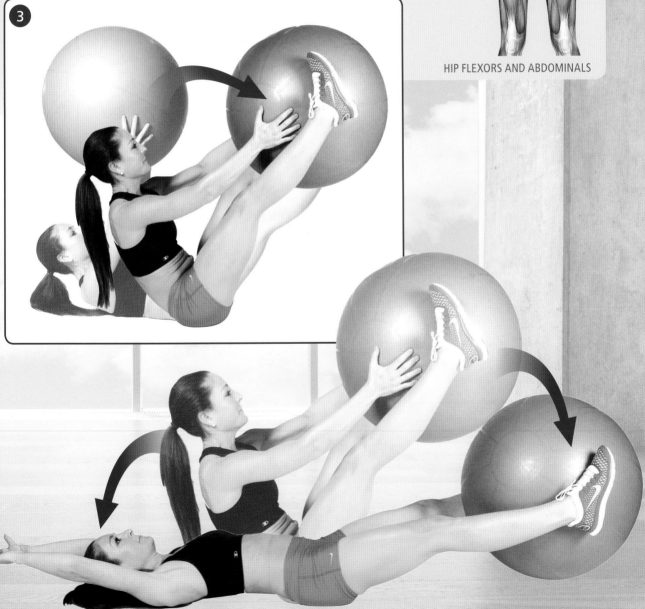

3

Swiss Ball Jackknife

The Swiss Ball Jackknife is a strength builder—primarily in the trunk and hips. For proper performance, you need to use coordination, timing, accuracy, and strength.

Step 1 Assume a push-up position with your arms shoulder-width apart and your shins resting on the Swiss ball.

Step 2 Bend your knees, rolling the ball in toward your chest, keeping your arms straight the whole time.

Step 3 Extend your legs and repeat for 20 repetitions.

CORRECT ACTION
- Keep a tight core throughout
- Proper breathing
- Keep your shoulders above your hands

AVOID
- A haphazard pattern
- Rounding your back
- Excessive speed

TARGET MUSCLES

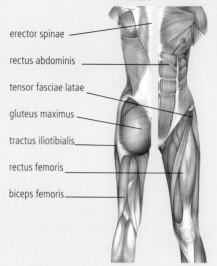

erector spinae
rectus abdominis
tensor fasciae latae
gluteus maximus
tractus iliotibialis
rectus femoris
biceps femoris

CORE AND HIPS   REAR   FRONT

Swiss Ball Forward Roll

The Swiss Ball Forward Roll is a key stabilizing exercise from which many movements can build. When holding this position, many of the key core muscles are activated. Recent studies have shown that the Swiss Ball Forward Roll activated more muscles in the rectus abdominis (the "six-pack muscle") and obliques than sit-ups and crunches.

Step 1 Kneel on the floor with your wrists resting on a Swiss ball, with your upper back straight and firmly supported, your feet shoulder-width apart, your hips raised, and your arms outstretched to your sides.

Step 2 Roll the ball forward slowly, until your elbows are over the center of the ball.

Step 3 Hold this position for five seconds, then slowly reverse the movement and repeat 10 times.

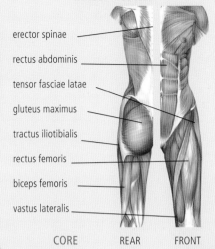

TARGET MUSCLES

erector spinae
rectus abdominis
tensor fasciae latae
gluteus maximus
tractus iliotibialis
rectus femoris
biceps femoris
vastus lateralis

CORE   REAR   FRONT

CORRECT ACTION
• Keep a tight core throughout the movement

AVOID
• A haphazard pattern
• Dropping your hips

T-Stabilization

The T-Stabilization is an exercise that benefits your core. It is especially effective for strengthening the abdominals, hips, and obliques.

Step 1 Start in the finished push-up position, with your arms extended to full lockout and your palms facing forward, supporting yourself on your toes.

Step 2 While keeping your body in one straight line, turn your left hip skyward, allowing your left foot to rest on the right. Raise your left arm laterally across your body until it points to the ceiling. Hold this position for 30 seconds (working up to 60 seconds). Return to the starting position, and repeat with the other side.

TARGET MUSCLES

rectus abdominis

obliques

transversus abdominis

tensor fasciae latae

sartorius

ABDOMINALS

CORRECT ACTION
• Keep your body in one straight line

AVOID
• Arching or bridging your back

Turkish Get-Up

The Turkish Get-Up is a simple but comprehensive routine that targets a wide range of muscles, including those in the shoulders, core, thighs, upper back, glutes, and triceps. It increases stability in the hips and aids balance throughout the body. Make it more of a challenge by holding a dumbbell or kettlebell in your raised hand.

Step 1 Lie flat on your back. Your right arm should be raised straight out above your chest, and your left arm should be at your side.

Step 2 Flex your right knee and place your right foot flat on the floor.

Step 3 Rotate your core slightly to the left and lift your shoulders off the floor, supporting your weight on your left forearm. Next, plant your left hand on the floor and lift yourself up to a sitting position.

Step 4 Lift your hips skyward and tuck your left leg under your body to support yourself on your left knee.

Step 5 Lift your left hand off the floor and push through your right foot to a standing position, keeping your right arm stretched over your head throughout the exercise.

Step 6 Return to the starting position. Perform 10 repetitions per arm.

CORRECT ACTION
- Keep a tight core throughout the movement

AVOID
- Performing the exercise at excessive speed

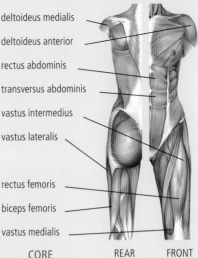

TARGET MUSCLES

- deltoideus medialis
- deltoideus anterior
- rectus abdominis
- transversus abdominis
- vastus intermedius
- vastus lateralis
- rectus femoris
- biceps femoris
- vastus medialis

CORE   REAR   FRONT

Chest Exercises

The fan-shaped chest muscles are responsible primarily for pulling the arms across the front of the body and for pushing objects away from the body. They are capable of lifting very heavy weights and are one of the more striking muscle complexes. Large developed pecs are generally associated with masculinity and raw power.

Swiss Ball Incline Dumbbell Press

Swiss Ball Incline Dumbbell Presses build and strengthen the often-neglected upper portion of the chest. They also recruit the core muscles to help with balance and stability. This makes for a fantastic functional and strengthening exercise.

Step 1 Begin lying with your back, head, and neck flat against a Swiss ball—keep your hips low to the ground for an incline effect. With your upper arms at 90 degrees to your torso, and resting on the ball, hold a pair of dumbbells shoulder-width apart.

Step 2 Clean the dumbbells to the upper and outer region of your shoulders and start by pressing up and inward until the dumbbells are nearly touching at the top.

Step 3 Arc out as you lower back down to the upper and outer portion of the shoulders and continue to complete 8 to 10 repetitions.

CORRECT ACTION
- Look for a controlled lowering
- Your heels should be pushed into the ground for proper stabilization
- Keep the dumbbells tight to the upper and outer region of your shoulders at the beginning and end of the exercise

AVOID
- Excessive speed
- Bouncing the dumbbells off your chest
- Arching your back

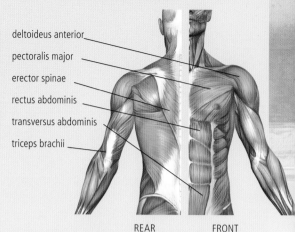

TARGET MUSCLES

deltoideus anterior
pectoralis major
erector spinae
rectus abdominis
transversus abdominis
triceps brachii

REAR   FRONT

CORE AND CHEST

Swiss Ball Flat Dumbbell Press

The Swiss Ball Flat Dumbbell Press is a slight variation on the incline press that also works on the chest, but this time the mid to lower section. However, the same core muscles are used for the routine.

Step 1 Start off sitting on a Swiss ball with a pair of dumbbells resting on your thighs.

Step 2 Move forward until your back is flat against the ball as well as your head and neck. Keep your glutes raised and your back flat.

Step 3 Clean the dumbbells to the mid and outer region of your shoulders and start by pressing up and inward until the dumbbells are nearly touching at the top.

Step 4 Arc out as you lower back down to the mid and outer portion of the shoulders and work for 8 to 10 repetitions.

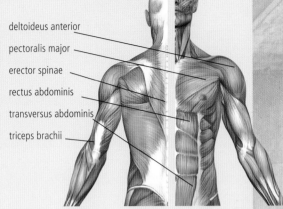

TARGET MUSCLES

- deltoideus anterior
- pectoralis major
- erector spinae
- rectus abdominis
- transversus abdominis
- triceps brachii

CORE AND CHEST   REAR   FRONT

CORRECT ACTION
- Look for a controlled lowering
- Keep your heels pushed into the ground for proper stabilization
- Keep the dumbbells tight to the mid and outer region of your shoulders at the beginning and end of the exercise

AVOID
- Excessive speed
- Bouncing the dumbbells off your chest
- Arching your back

Swiss Ball Dumbbell Fly

The Swiss Ball Dumbbell Fly works all the upper body, not just the pectoral muscles. Those with weak shoulders should exercise caution, as this exercise may place stress upon this area.

Step 1 Start by lying back on a Swiss ball, holding a pair of dumbbells at arm's length above you.

Step 2 Move your arms outward until your pectorals are fully elongated.

Step 3 Reverse the motion by squeezing your arms back together and bringing the dumbbells to their original position for 10 repetitions.

CORRECT ACTION
- Look for slow and controlled repetitions
- Keep your core tight and your body elongated
- Perform the movement in a slow and controlled manner

AVOID
- Allowing the lower back to dip too far
- Excessive speed
- Too great a stretch

TARGET MUSCLES

deltoideus anterior
pectoralis major
erector spinae
rhomboideus major
rectus abdominis
triceps brachii
extensor digitorum
gluteus maximus

CORE   REAR   FRONT

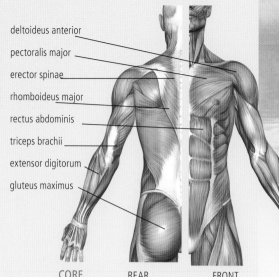

Perfect Push-Up

Perhaps no other single upper-body exercise can do more for upper-body strength and conditioning than the iconic push-up. Touching on just about every major muscle group of the upper body, this mainstay body-weight exercise even utilizes some of the lower-body muscles.

Step 1 Begin in a facedown position on your toes with your ams straight and your hands shoulder-width apart, holding a pair of rotating handles.

Step 2 Lower yourself until your upper arms are parallel to the ground. Then push your arms to full extension.

Step 3 Keep your core engaged and your body in a straight line as you lower again to complete 12 to 15 repetitions.

CORRECT ACTION
- Look for slow and controlled repetitions
- Keep your torso stabilized and your upper body straight
- At the lowest point, your upper arms should be parallel to the ground

AVOID
- Excessive speed
- Shallow or bouncy repetitions
- Allowing the lower back to dip too far

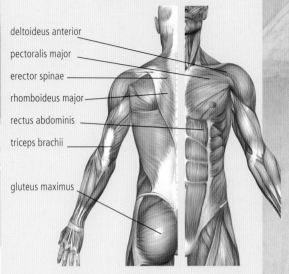

TARGET MUSCLES

deltoideus anterior
pectoralis major
erector spinae
rhomboideus major
rectus abdominis
triceps brachii
gluteus maximus

CORE   REAR   FRONT

Decline Push-Up

This advanced body-weight exercise is a more challenging variation of the straightforward push-up. It develops virtually every upper-body muscle group as well as some of the muscles in the lower body. The exercise works the muscles that stabilize the shoulders more effectively than a regular push-up. You can use a flat bench instead of a Swiss ball.

Step 1 Begin by placing your feet on a Swiss ball while assuming a facedown position with your hands planted shoulder-width apart, directly beneath your chest.

Step 2 Lower yourself until your upper arms are parallel to the ground. Then push your arms to full extension.

Step 3 Keep your core engaged and your body in a straight line as you lower again and continue to complete 12 to 15 repetitions.

TARGET MUSCLES

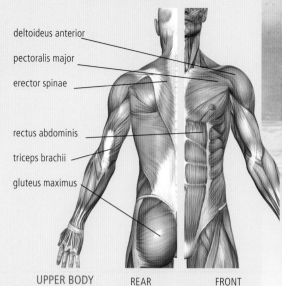

- deltoideus anterior
- pectoralis major
- erector spinae
- rectus abdominis
- triceps brachii
- gluteus maximus

UPPER BODY   REAR   FRONT

CORRECT ACTION
- Strive for slow and controlled repetitions
- Keep your torso stabilized and your upper body straight

AVOID
- Excessive speed
- Shallow or bouncy repetitions
- Allowing the lower back to dip too far

Single-Arm Medicine Ball Push-Up

The Single-Arm Medicine Ball Push-Up goes beyond the traditional push-up in relation to strength, range of motion, balance, and stability. The practitioner is constantly moving while working most of the muscles of the upper body, as well as some of the muscles located below.

Step 1 Start in a facedown position on your toes with your hands planted shoulder-width apart, directly beneath your chest. Place a medicine ball beneath one of your hands.

Step 2 Start by lowering yourself until your upper arms are parallel to the ground. Then push your arms to full extension.

Step 3 Once at the top, pass the ball to the other hand and perform the movement again.

Step 4 Keep your core engaged and your body straight as you pass the ball back and forth at the top portion of the movement for 12 to 15 repetitions.

TARGET MUSCLES

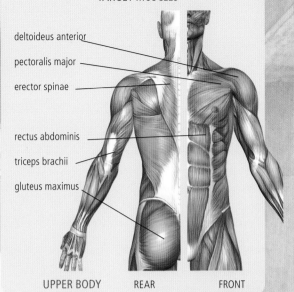

deltoideus anterior
pectoralis major
erector spinae
rectus abdominis
triceps brachii
gluteus maximus

UPPER BODY   REAR   FRONT

CORRECT ACTION
- Look for slow and controlled repetitions
- Keep your torso stabilized and your upper body straight

AVOID
- Excessive speed
- Shallow or bouncy repetitions
- Allowing the lower back to dip too far

Barbell Bench Press

Arguably the best-known of all equipment-based exercises, the Barbell Bench Press has been responsible for improvements in chest strength and development the world over. A classic chest routine, it works many of the major upper-body muscle groups.

Step 1 Start by lying back on a flat bench with your feet planted shoulder-width apart on the ground. Your hands should assume an overhand grip on a barbell, a few inches beyond shoulder-width apart.

Step 2 Unrack the barbell and lower it to your nipple line, touching your chest and then exhaling as you push the barbell up to a full lockout.

Step 3 Lower and work for 8 to 10 repetitions.

CORRECT ACTION
- Strive for a controlled lowering
- Keep your heels pushed into the ground for proper stabilization
- Look for repetition fluidity

AVOID
- Excessive speed
- Bouncing the bar off your chest
- Arching your back

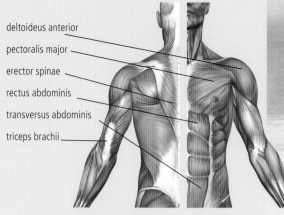

TARGET MUSCLES

deltoideus anterior
pectoralis major
erector spinae
rectus abdominis
transversus abdominis
triceps brachii

CHEST   REAR   FRONT

Lateral Shoulder Raise

The Lateral Shoulder Raise is a key routine for building shoulder mass and width. It is especially effective at strengthening the medial deltoid in the center of your shoulders, and is one of the few exercises to isolate this muscle.

Step 1 Begin by standing straight with a pair of dumbbells in your hands, positioned down at waist height.

Step 2 Slowly move the dumbdells up in an outward motion until they are above shoulder height, in line with your head.

Step 3 Bring the dumbbells back down so they are back in their original position. Continue to complete 10 to 12 repetitions.

TARGET MUSCLES

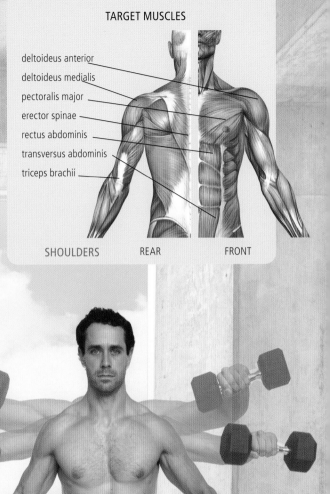

deltoideus anterior
deltoideus medialis
pectoralis major
erector spinae
rectus abdominis
transversus abdominis
triceps brachii

SHOULDERS   REAR   FRONT

1

CORRECT ACTION
- Look for a controlled movement
- Keep your elbows straight

AVOID
- LIfting the dumbbells above your head

Hand Weight Push-Up

The Hand Weight Push-Up from the floor goes a step beyond a push-up in that you are actually crunching at the top of the movement as well as forcing your upper body to rise up from the floor. In this regard, it is both a strengthening and a functional exercise, concentrating less on individual muscles and more on making them work together.

Step 1 Begin in a facedown position on your toes with your ams straight and your hands shoulder-width apart, resting your weight on a pair of hand weights or kettlebells.

Step 2 Lower yourself until your upper arms are parallel to the ground. Then push your arms to full extension.

Step 3 Keep your core engaged and your body in a straight line as you lower again to complete 12 to 15 repetitions.

1

TARGET MUSCLES

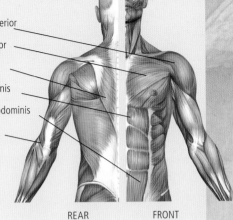

deltoideus anterior

pectoralis major

erector spinae

rectus abdominis

transversus abdominis

triceps brachii

REAR   FRONT

CHEST AND TRICEPS

CORRECT ACTION
- Look for a full pressed extension lined up with your mid-chest
- Strive to use your abdominals
- Keep your forearms stable

AVOID
- Excessive speed
- The weights tipping forward

2

Plyo Kettlebell Push-Up

The Plyo Kettlebell Push-Up targets the pectorals, shoulders, and triceps. Its main aim is to increase strength in the chest.

Step 1 Assume a classic push-up position, on your toes, with one hand planted on the floor and the other gripping a kettlebell. Lower yourself until your upper arms are parallel to the floor.

Step 2 Quickly push your arms to full extension. As you do so, switch hands on the kettlebell.

Step 3 Lower yourself again, switching sides each time you push yourself back up. Complete 8 to 10 push-ups on each side.

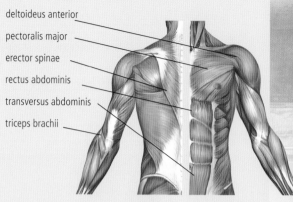

TARGET MUSCLES

- deltoideus anterior
- pectoralis major
- erector spinae
- rectus abdominis
- transversus abdominis
- triceps brachii

REAR   FRONT

CORE

CORRECT ACTION
- Keep your back flat throughout the movement

AVOID
- Bouncing excessively and using momentum

MODIFICATIONS

Easier: Keep the same hand planted on the kettlebell.

More difficult: Perform the push-ups with both hands gripping kettlebells (right).

Plyometric Push-Up

A further variation on the conventional push-up, the Plyometric Push-Up is aimed at the pectorals, deltoids, triceps, upper back, and core. It produces explosive power in the upper body. Variations include performing it without clapping, or adding resistance weights to your wrists.

Step 1 Start in a standard push-up position.

Step 2 Lower yourself until your upper arms are parallel to the floor, then prepare to return to the starting position.

Step 3 As you push up, quickly clap your hands together before safely touching them back to the floor. Perform 15 repetitions.

CORRECT ACTION
• Keep a tight core throughout the movement

AVOID
• Putting excessive strain on your wrists

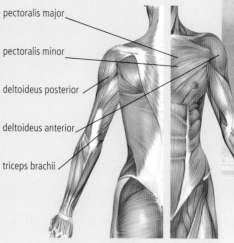

TARGET MUSCLES

pectoralis major

pectoralis minor

deltoideus posterior

deltoideus anterior

triceps brachii

CHEST AND SHOULDERS

Resistance Bars

Resistance (or flex) bars have been around for decades. They provide a great upper-body exercise—isometric holds deliver intense resistance to multiple muscle groups, working your shoulders, arms (forearms and triceps in particular), back, and chest.

Step 1 Stand with your feet firmly planted, hip-width apart.

Step 2 Hold the handles of the bar in each hand. Keep the bar straight, level with your chest.

Step 3 Slowly bend the bar into a U shape, until the handles almost touch. Hold for three seconds.

Step 4 Slowly release the bar back to its straight position.

Step 5 Repeat 20 times.

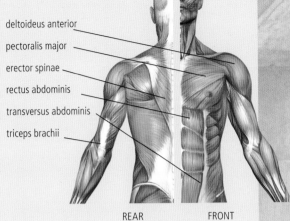

TARGET MUSCLES

deltoideus anterior

pectoralis major

erector spinae

rectus abdominis

transversus abdominis

triceps brachii

REAR   FRONT

CORE

CORRECT ACTION
- Keep your arm and chest muscles tensed throughout the motion
- For best results, it is important to perform the exercise as slowly as you can

AVOID
- Letting the bar "snap" back into position

Shoulder Exercises

The shoulder is an intricate series of muscles—principally the deltoids—responsible for the 360-degree rotation of the arms. Many gym users have heavily developed front deltoids as a result of their use in the many forms of press routines. However, they often neglect the lateral and posterior sections due to the lighter weights involved. A fully developed set of shoulders not only aids strength and develops the aesthetics of a physique, but it also improves posture.

Dumbbell Power Clean

The Dumbbell Power Clean is a multijoint exercise that increases raw power, size, and strength throughout the shoulder girdle and upper back. It also enhances the three-dimensional aspect of one's physique by offering depth and dimension.

Step 1 Begin by standing behind a pair of dumbbells.

Step 2 Squat down and grab the dumbbells with a wide, overhand grip and your feet shoulder-width apart.

Step 3 Flip the dumbbells up until they are nearly touching your upper chest, then reverse and return to the starting position.

Step 4 Continue to complete 6 to 8 repetitions.

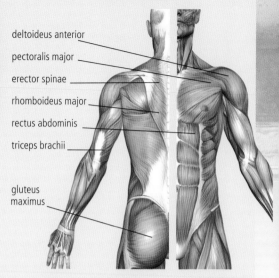

TARGET MUSCLES

deltoideus anterior
pectoralis major
erector spinae
rhomboideus major
rectus abdominis
triceps brachii

gluteus maximus

REAR   FRONT
SHOULDERS AND UPPER BACK

CORRECT ACTION
- Keep the dumbbells close to your body
- Maintain a straight back

AVOID
- Placing too much stress on your wrists
- Excessive momentum

2

3

Dumbbell Power Clean and Press

The Dumbbell Power Clean and Press works many of the major upper-body muscles but also adds dimension and raw power to one's physique. It is an advanced movement that requires strength, timing, momentum, and technique to derive the most from it.

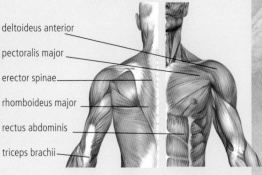

TARGET MUSCLES

deltoideus anterior
pectoralis major
erector spinae
rhomboideus major
rectus abdominis
triceps brachii

REAR   FRONT

SHOULDERS AND UPPER BACK

Step 1 Stand behind a pair of dumbbells.

Step 2 Squat down and pick them up with a wide, overhand grip and your feet shoulder-width apart.

Step 3 Flip the dumbbells until they almost touch your upper chest, push to full lockout directly overhead, then reverse and return to the starting position.

Step 4 Continue to complete 6 to 8 repetitions.

CORRECT ACTION
• Make sure the dumbbells remain close to your body
• Keep a straight back

AVOID
• Too much stress on your wrists
• Excessive momentum

2

3

Kettlebell Double Clean

You should learn how to clean with a set of very light kettlebells. Keep your arms loose, with just enough tension to perform the exercise. However, your body should be locked tight and braced. Using a lighter pair of kettlebells will allow you to put all your focus on the swing and redirection, rather than on just getting the kettlebell into place. You can also add a press to the movement, raising the kettlebells above your head at the end of the motion.

WARNING Not advisable if you have wrist pain or shoulder issues.

Step 1 Start in a squat position, with a kettlebell in each hand. The midpoint of the handles should be aligned with the midpoint of your feet.

Step 2 Internally rotate your arms as you reach down so that when you hold the handles your thumbs are pointing back behind your legs.

Step 3 Tense your abdominals, drive your feet into the floor, and thrust your hips forward to create the momentum required to clean the kettlebells up into the rack position.

Step 4 Once the kettlebells are in motion, loosen your grip to allow the kettlebells to wrap around your forearms as they slide into position.

Step 5 Repeat 15 times.

CORRECT ACTION
- Keep your eyes forward to help keep your body squared and back straight
- Your neck should be elongated
- Use tight, controlled exhalation

AVOID
- Letting the kettlebells hit your forearms

TARGET MUSCLES

deltoideus anterior

pectoralis major

erector spinae

rhomboideus major

rectus abdominis

triceps brachii

gluteus maximus

SHOULDERS AND UPPER BACK

Dumbbell Shoulder Press

The Dumbbell Shoulder Press is an outstanding shoulder-strengthening exercise. In some aspects it is superior to its barbell equivalent, as it allows the dumbbells to arc in and out during the execution of the movement.

Step 1 Begin with a pair of dumbbells cleaned to your outer shoulders, with your palms facing forward.

Step 2 Start by pressing upward and inward in an arc so that the dumbbells are nearly touching at the top, then lower down the same pathway.

Step 3 Complete 8 to 10 repetitions.

TARGET MUSCLES

- deltoideus anterior
- trapezius
- pectoralis major
- erector spinae
- rhomboideus major
- rectus abdominis
- triceps brachii

SHOULDERS AND
UPPER BACK

CORRECT ACTION
- Strive for slow and controlled repetitions
- Keep your torso stabilized and your upper body straight
- Lower the dumbbells close to the outside of the shoulders

AVOID
- Bouncy repetitions
- Allowing the dumbbells to drop during the downward phase
- Lacking a full range of motion

Alternate Swiss Ball Dumbbell Shoulder Press

The Alternate Swiss Ball Dumbbell Shoulder Press not only strengthens the deltoids, but also works the entire core due to its stabilization demands. It is a lesson in both balance and power.

Step 1 Begin in a seated position on a Swiss ball with a pair of dumbbells cleaned to your outer shoulders.

Step 2 Start by pressing one dumbbell upward to full overhead extension and then lower it back down to the starting position.

Step 3 Follow through with the opposite arm and continue back and forth for 8 to 10 repetitions per arm.

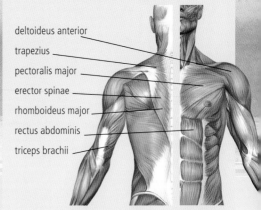

TARGET MUSCLES

deltoideus anterior
trapezius
pectoralis major
erector spinae
rhomboideus major
rectus abdominis
triceps brachii

REAR   FRONT
SHOULDERS

CORRECT ACTION
- Look for slow and controlled repetitions
- Keep your torso stabilized and your upper body straight
- Lower the dumbbells close to the outside of the shoulders

AVOID
- Bouncy repetitions
- Allowing the dumbbells to drop during the downward phase
- Lacking a full range of motion

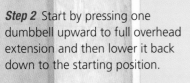

Alternate Shoulder Press

The Alternate Shoulder Press is another straightforward routine that focuses on the deltoids. Its stabilization and movement patterns mean that the exercise also works to strengthen the core.

Step 1 Start by standing with a pair of dumbbells cleaned to your outer shoulders.

Step 2 Lift your right arm up so that the dumbbell is directly overhead.

Step 3 Lower and repeat with the other arm. Complete 8 to 10 repetitions per arm.

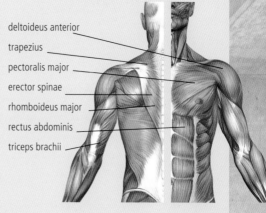

TARGET MUSCLES

- deltoideus anterior
- trapezius
- pectoralis major
- erector spinae
- rhomboideus major
- rectus abdominis
- triceps brachii

REAR   FRONT

SHOULDERS

CORRECT ACTION
- Aim for slow and controlled repetitions
- Maintain a straight upper body
- Keep the dumbbells close to your body

AVOID
- Overarching your back
- Excessive speed or momentum
- Lacking a full range of motion

Front Raise

The Front Raise effectively isolates the anterior, or front part, of the shoulder, resulting in a stronger and more delineated frontal region. It is most effective for those who have difficulty performing overhead pressing. You can also perform this as an Alternating Front Raise, raising and lowering each arm in sequence.

Step 1 Begin in a standing position, holding a pair of dumbbells at your sides with your palms facing each other.

Step 2 Raise your arms upward. Rotate your palms so they are facedown at the top of the movement and your arms are parallel to the ground.

Step 3 Complete 8 to 10 repetitions.

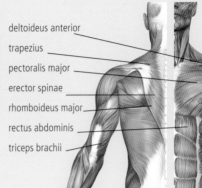

TARGET MUSCLES

- deltoideus anterior
- trapezius
- pectoralis major
- erector spinae
- rhomboideus major
- rectus abdominis
- triceps brachii

REAR   FRONT

SHOULDERS

CORRECT ACTION
- Maintain an upright stance throughout the exercise
- Arms slightly bent throughout the movement
- Your palms rotate downward as you raise your arms

AVOID
- Raising your arms above parallel to the ground
- Excessive speed or momentum
- Allowing the lower back to take over the movement

Lateral Raise

The Lateral Raise strengthens the deltoids, but also makes the shoulders appear wider. Its location at the side means that the small deltoid muscle can contribute to the desired V-taper of the practitioner.

Step 1 Start off in a standing position with a pair of dumbbells in hand and hanging at your sides, palms facing your thighs.

Step 2 Raise your arms directly out to the sides, with slightly bent arms, and turn the thumbs slightly downward as you raise your arms parallel to the ground.

Step 3 Lower and continue to complete 10 to 12 repetitions.

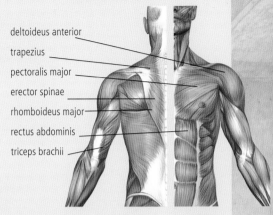

TARGET MUSCLES

deltoideus anterior
trapezius
pectoralis major
erector spinae
rhomboideus major
rectus abdominis
triceps brachii

REAR   FRONT

SHOULDERS

CORRECT ACTION
- Maintain your posture throughout the exercise
- Keep your arms slightly bent throughout the movement
- Have your thumbs pointed slightly downward as you raise your arms

AVOID
- Raising above parallel to the ground
- Excessive speed or momentum
- Allowing the anterior deltoids to take over the movement

Bent-Over Lateral Raise

Although not one of the most glamorous exercises, the Bent-Over Lateral Raise is nevertheless an important routine for developing the shoulder region. It also assists in promoting good posture.

Step 1 Begin in a standing position with a pair of dumbbells in hand and hanging at your sides, palms facing each other.

Step 2 Bend your knees slightly, lean forward at the waist, and stick your rear out while holding the dumbbells out at your sides.

Step 3 Raise your slightly bent arms directly out to the sides in a reverse hugging motion, then lower and complete 10 to 12 repetitions.

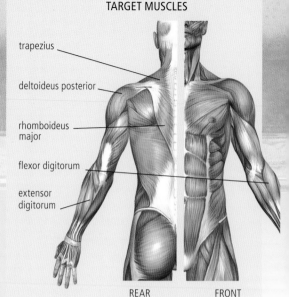

TARGET MUSCLES

trapezius

deltoideus posterior

rhomboideus major

flexor digitorum

extensor digitorum

REAR   FRONT

SHOULDERS

CORRECT ACTION
- Maintain a flat back throughout the exercise
- Keep your arms slightly bent

AVOID
- Excessive speed or momentum
- Allowing the anterior deltoids to take over the movement
- Rounding your back

Alternating Kettlebell Press

The Alternating Kettlebell Press works on the deltoids and triceps. It is a simple but effective way of building shoulder strength.

Step 1 Stand with your feet shoulder-width apart and a pair of kettlebells cleaned to the sides of your shoulders. Your palms should be facing inward.

Step 2 Raise the right kettlebell directly overhead until your arm locks out, turning your palm forward in mid-motion. Keep the other kettlebell as still as possible.

Step 3 Lower your right arm, turning your palm back toward you as you do so, then complete the same movement with the left arm. Perform 8 to 10 repetitions per arm.

TARGET MUSCLES

deltoideus posterior

deltoideus medialis

deltoideus anterior

triceps

REAR   FRONT

SHOULDERS

CORRECT ACTION
- Keep your core engaged and straight on

AVOID
- Leaning back too far when executing the movement

MODIFICATIONS

Easier: Press with both arms at the same time (below).

More difficult: Raise one leg off the floor for a tougher challenge.

Dumbbell Shrug

The Dumbbell Shrug is a superb trapezius strengthener and also adds raw size to the powerful upper back complex. A favorite in many gyms, it is right up there with bench presses and barbell curls in terms of popularity.

Step 1 Begin by picking up a pair of dumbbells and letting them hang at your sides with your palms facing each another.

Step 2 Shrug your shoulders straight up toward your ears. Then return to the starting position for 10 to 12 repetitions.

TARGET MUSCLES

semispinalis

trapezius

pectoralis major

erector spinae

rhomboideus major

rectus abdominis

flexor digitorum

extensor digitorum

NECK

CORRECT ACTION
- Shrug straight up and down
- Keep your head slightly forward
- Strive for a controlled lowering of the weight

AVOID
- Rolling your shoulders backward
- Excessive speed or momentum
- Leaning backward

1

2

Overhead Dumbbell Shrug

The Overhead Dumbbell Shrug is a unique version of the traditional shrug that completes the powerful upper back and shoulder complexes. Although you cannot perform this exercise as forcefully as a standard shrug, the movement is fresh enough to offer additional muscle stimulation.

Step 1 Pick up a pair of dumbbells with your knuckles facing forward and push them directly overhead until your arms lock.

Step 2 Shrug your shoulders straight up toward your ears, then return to the starting position.

Step 3 Complete 10 to 12 repetitions.

CORRECT ACTION
- Shrug directly up and down
- Keep your arms elongated
- Maintain proper posture throughout

AVOID
- Rolling your shoulders backward
- Excessive speed or momentum
- Leaning backward

TARGET MUSCLES

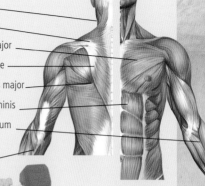

- semispinalis
- trapezius
- pectoralis major
- erector spinae
- rhomboideus major
- rectus abdominis
- flexor digitorum
- extensor digitorum

NECK

Barbell Power Clean

The Barbell Power Clean is a classic routine for the deltoids, upper back, thighs, glutes, hamstrings, and core. It increases power and mass in the shoulders and upper back region.

Step 1 Stand in front of a barbell with your feet shoulder-width apart. Looking straight ahead, squat down and grab the barbell with a wide overhand grip. Your knees should be close to the bar.

Step 2 Straighten your legs to return to a standing position. As you do so, flip the bar until it is nearly touching your upper chest.

Step 3 From the upper chest, reverse your flip and return to the starting position. Complete 6 to 8 repetitions.

TARGET MUSCLES

trapezius

subscapularis

deltoideus posterior

deltoideus medialis

gluteus maximus

deltoideus anterior

infraspinatus

teres minor

teres major

REAR   FRONT

SHOULDERS AND UPPER BACK

CORRECT ACTION
• Be sure to use your legs to help with the movement

AVOID
• Overarching your back

②

MODIFICATIONS

Easier: Use a very light bar or just your own body weight.

More difficult: Use dumbbells instead of a barbell (above).

Double Kettlebell Snatch

The Double Kettlebell Snatch builds up strength in the deltoids, glutes, quads, and hamstrings. An easier variation is to only use one kettlebell and lift it with both hands. For more of a challenge, alternate the arms, so that you lift one kettlebell at a time.

Step 1 Stand with your feet a little more than shoulder-width apart, holding a pair of kettlebells at your sides.

Step 2 Squat down, leaning forward slightly and sticking out your behind. Bring your arms between your legs, so that the kettlebells are next to your inner thighs.

Step 3 In one swift and determined movement, drive through your hips and swing the kettlebells overhead. Lower and repeat 8 to 10 times.

TARGET MUSCLES

deltoideus posterior

deltoideus medialis

deltoideus anterior

REAR   FRONT

SHOULDERS

CORRECT ACTION
- Keep your back straight throughout the movement

AVOID
- Rolling your shoulders backward
- Excessive speed or momentum
- Leaning backward
- Powering through the movement and overusing your shoulders

External Rotation with Band

The External Rotation with Band is a simple routine to increase power and strength in the shoulder muscles. It is also useful for boosting your triceps and forearms.

Step 1 Fasten one end of a band around a post at elbow height. Grasp the other end with your right hand, keeping your upper arm pressed against your side and your forearm parallel to the ground.

Step 2 Keeping your upper arm in position, move your forearm as far out to the side as you can before returning to the starting position. Complete 12 to 15 repetitions, then switch to the other arm.

CORRECT ACTION
• Keep your upper arm against your side

AVOID
• Working at an excessively fast pace

TARGET MUSCLES

deltoideus posterior

deltoideus medialis

deltoideus anterior

REAR | FRONT
SHOULDERS

Shoulder Press with Medicine Ball

The Shoulder Press with Medicine Ball is a simple but effective routine to build shoulder strength. To add some variety, you can execute the exercise by standing on one leg or even with your eyes closed.

Step 1 Stand with your feet shoulder-width apart and a medicine ball in your right hand at head height.

Step 2 Extend your right arm up as far as it will go, pushing the medicine ball up above your head.

Step 3 Lower the medicine ball back to head height. Perform 12 to 15 repetitions, then switch to the left arm.

CORRECT ACTION
• Keep your spine straight throughout the routine

AVOID
• Excessive speed or momentum

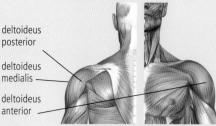

TARGET MUSCLES

deltoideus posterior
deltoideus medialis
deltoideus anterior

REAR   FRONT

SHOULDERS

Standing Barbell Press

Another classic equipment-based routine, the explosive Standing Barbell Press increases mass in the shoulders and upper arms, especially the deltoids and triceps.

Step 1 Stand in front of a barbell, situated at eye level on a power rack. Grab the barbell with an overhand grip that is shoulder-width apart, and walk back with it.

Step 2 Extend your arms, pushing the barbell overhead, from your upper chest to arm's length.

Step 3 Lower the barbell back to your upper chest. Perform 6 to 8 repetitions.

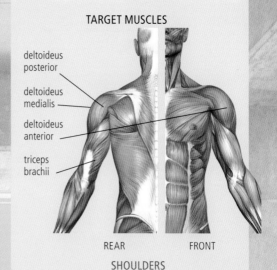

TARGET MUSCLES

deltoideus posterior

deltoideus medialis

deltoideus anterior

triceps brachii

REAR   FRONT

SHOULDERS

CORRECT ACTION
- Always press to the front of the shoulders, never behind your neck

AVOID
- Leaning back excessively

MODIFICATIONS

Easier: Use a very light bar or just your own body weight.

More difficult: Use dumbbells (left) instead of a barbell.

Arm Exercises

The main muscles in the arms are the two-headed biceps and three-headed triceps. Responsible for the inward turning of the wrist, the biceps are at the front of the upper arm and are arguably the most high-profile muscles in strength training. The triceps work in opposition to the biceps, turning the wrist outward. Since the triceps make up two-thirds of your upper-arm circumference, they are actually more important to building "big arms" than the biceps.

EZ Bar Lying Triceps Extensions

EZ Bar Triceps Extensions, or "skull-crushers" as they are affectionately known, are a primary strength routine for the triceps. A highly effective mass builder, they are to the upper arms what squats are to the thighs.

Step 1 Begin by lying back on a flat bench, with an inside, overhand grip on an EZ curl bar and your feet flat on the floor for support.

Step 2 Press the bar above your chest to full lockout and then bend your arms backward at the elbow joint, to past your head.

Step 3 Keeping your elbows in and locked, extend the bar back up to full lockout.

Step 4 Continue to complete 10 to 12 repetitions.

CORRECT ACTION
- Look for a full stretch behind your head
- Keep your torso stabilized and your upper body straight
- Keep your elbows in

AVOID
- Excessive speed
- Knocking yourself in the head
- Flared elbows

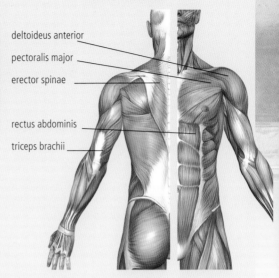

TARGET MUSCLES

deltoideus anterior
pectoralis major
erector spinae
rectus abdominis
triceps brachii

REAR   FRONT
TRICEPS

Swiss Ball Overhead Dumbbell Extensions

Swiss Ball Overhead Dumbbell Extensions are a particularly effective way of developing the substantial and strong outer section of the triceps muscles. Performing these extensions on a Swiss ball brings the core further into play.

Step 1 Start by sitting on a Swiss ball with a pair of dumbbells held above your head, with your palms facing up and your elbows in.

Step 2 Bend your forearms back behind your head to approximately 90 degrees, then extend them back above your head.

Step 3 Work for 10 to 12 repetitions.

CORRECT ACTION
- Aim for slow and controlled repetitions
- Keep your elbows in
- Keep your upper body still

AVOID
- Excessive speed
- Shallow or bouncy repetitions
- Hitting your head

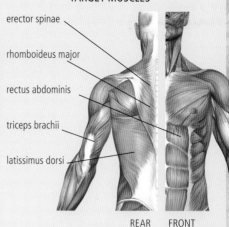

TARGET MUSCLES

erector spinae

rhomboideus major

rectus abdominis

triceps brachii

latissimus dorsi

REAR   FRONT

TRICEPS

Band Curls

Band Curls are a good finishing routine for the biceps, flushing them with an extra pump in the arms. These curls also double as an effective shape-enhancing exercise.

Step 1 Fasten a band either to a stable object or under your feet and hold the ends in both hands, with your palms facing upward.

Step 2 Bend at the elbows until your hands are nearly touching your shoulders.

Step 3 Return to the starting position and continue to complete 12 to 15 repetitions.

CORRECT ACTION
- Look for a full and complete range of motion
- Secure the band properly
- Aim for a controlled lowering of resistance

AVOID
- A shortened range of motion
- Excessive speed or momentum
- Using your lower back excessively

TARGET MUSCLES

erector spinae

biceps brachii

rectus abdominis

flexor digitorum

extensor digitorum

REAR   FRONT

BICEPS

1

2

Overhead Triceps Extensions

Overhead Triceps Extensions are a great exercise to finish or flush the triceps. They are particularly successful at isolating the triceps, helping to enhance the shape of this complex, three-headed muscle. This exercise can also be performed with a cable stack.

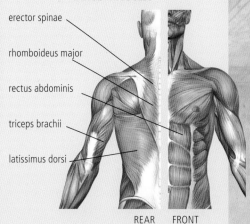

TARGET MUSCLES

erector spinae

rhomboideus major

rectus abdominis

triceps brachii

latissimus dorsi

REAR   FRONT

TRICEPS

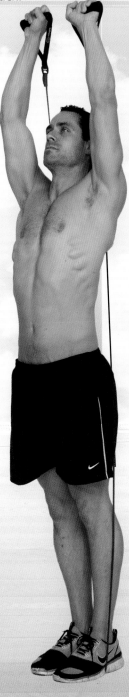

Step 1 Fasten a band either to a stable object or under your feet and hold the ends in both hands behind your head.

Step 2 Extend your forearms forward to their full length above your head while keeping your upper arms braced.

Step 3 Return back to the starting position and complete 12 to 15 repetitions.

CORRECT ACTION
• Look for slow and controlled repetitions
• Keep your elbows in
• Keep your upper body still

AVOID
• Excessive speed
• Extending too low through the movement
• Hitting your head

Band Kickbacks

Band Kickbacks are another excellent finishing movement for the triceps. They help to delineate the horseshoe-like shape of the muscle as well as keeping constant tension on the movement throughout the exercise.

Step 1 Hold one end of a band in each hand while stepping in the middle to provide tension.

Step 2 Lean forward, while maintaining a flat back, with your upper arms glued to your sides and your elbows in as you extend the forearms to a straight line behind you.

Step 3 Contract, then return to the starting position and continue to complete 12 to 15 repetitions.

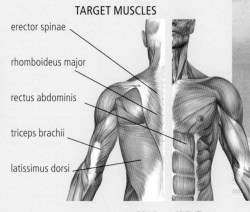

TARGET MUSCLES

erector spinae

rhomboideus major

rectus abdominis

triceps brachii

latissimus dorsi

REAR   FRONT

TRICEPS

CORRECT ACTION
- Look for slow and controlled repetitions
- Keep your elbows in
- Keep your back flat

AVOID
- Excessive speed
- Allowing your elbows to flare outward
- A shortened range of motion

Swiss Ball Preacher Curls

Swiss Ball Preacher Curls are an effective exercise for working the biceps, particularly the lower portion of the muscle that inserts at the flexor muscles. The Swiss ball adds a further dimension by bringing the stabilizing powers of the core into play while executing the movement.

Step 1 Sit on a Swiss ball and make an underhand, shoulder-width grip on a barbell at arm's length.

Step 2 Bend at the elbows until your palms are nearly touching your shoulders. Return to the starting position and complete 10 to 12 repetitions.

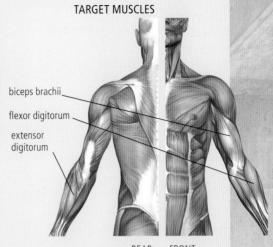

TARGET MUSCLES

biceps brachii

flexor digitorum

extensor digitorum

REAR   FRONT

BICEPS

CORRECT ACTION
- Look for a full and complete range of motion
- Keep your arms straight out in front of you
- Aim for a controlled lowering of the weight

AVOID
- Swinging the weight up
- Excessive speed or momentum
- Using your shoulders excessively

1

2

Assisted Dips

Assisted Dips are a highly effective strengthening exercise. They are perfect for applying constant tension to the triceps and have the additional benefit of core stabilization during motion. They are easier than normal Dips in that you don't have to lift your whole body weight.

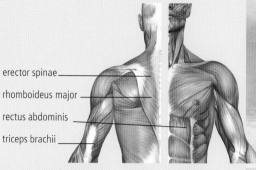

TARGET MUSCLES

erector spinae

rhomboideus major

rectus abdominis

triceps brachii

REAR   FRONT

TRICEPS

Step 1 Begin by standing in front of a dipping station.

Step 2 Taking a close grip on the bars, lower yourself forward, with your elbows at your sides, until your forearms are at least parallel to the ground, lower if possible.

Step 3 Push straight down until your arms are fully extended, then slowly bend the arms back. Complete 10 to 12 repetitions.

CORRECT ACTION
- Look for slow and controlled repetitions
- Keep your elbows in at your sides
- Aim for a full and complete range of motion

AVOID
- Excessive speed
- Shallow or bouncy repetitions
- Leaning too far forward

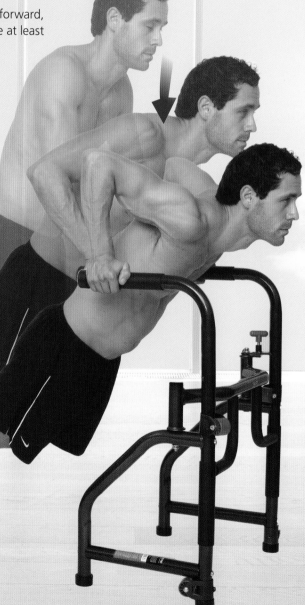

Incline EZ Bar Curls

The main benefit of Incline EZ Bar Curls is quite simply that you cannot cheat or swing through the movement. The routine allows the practitioner to be locked into a preselected range of motion and effectively isolates the intended muscle.

Step 1 Begin by leaning over the back of an incline bench while holding an EZ bar. Place your upper arms firmly on the upper surface of the bench with your chest braced against the top edge of the pad and your knees bent.

Step 2 While holding the EZ bar at full extension below you, bend at the elbows until your palms are nearly touching your shoulders. Return to the starting position for 10 to 12 repetitions.

TARGET MUSCLES

biceps brachii
flexor digitorum
extensor digitorum

REAR   FRONT

BICEPS

CORRECT ACTION
- Look for a full and complete range of motion
- Hold your arms straight out in front of you
- Lower the weight in a controlled manner

AVOID
- Swinging the weight up
- Excessive speed or momentum
- Using your shoulders excessively

Vertical Dips

Vertical Dips are a fantastic triceps strengthener, but they also work the entire upper body. An explosive movement, the Vertical Dip is a well-established exercise that repays its practitioner big dividends.

Step 1 Begin by standing in front of a vertical dip station with your hands placed firmly on the parallel bars.

Step 2 Lower yourself and take a deep breath as you bend your upper arms until your triceps are parallel to the ground.

Step 3 Exhale as you push yourself back up to lockout.

Step 4 Continue to complete 8 to 10 full repetitions.

CORRECT ACTION
- Look for slow and controlled repetitions
- Keep your torso stabilized and your upper body straight
- Lower yourself until your upper arms are parallel to the ground

AVOID
- Excessive speed
- Shallow or bouncy repetitions
- Leaning too far forward

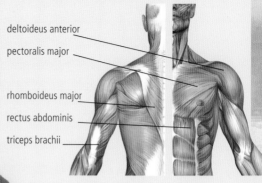

TARGET MUSCLES

deltoideus anterior

pectoralis major

rhomboideus major

rectus abdominis

triceps brachii

REAR   FRONT

TRICEPS

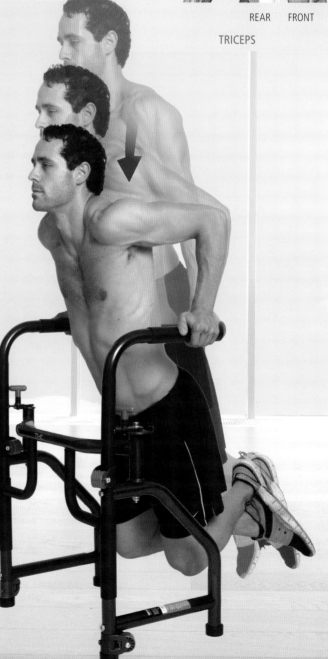

Bench Dips

Bench Dips are an old standby exercise, a fun and effective triceps strength builder that also prepares a person for body-weight exercises. When the range of motion makes a complete repetition impossible to perform, there is little risk of hurting yourself, as the set can be ceased immediately.

Step 1 Begin by sitting in the middle of a flat bench, facing sideways.

Step 2 Place your hands next to your hips. Lower yourself and take a deep breath as you bend your upper arms until your triceps are parallel to the ground.

Step 3 Exhale as you push yourself back up to lockout.

Step 4 Continue to complete 8 to 10 full repetitions.

CORRECT ACTION
- Look for slow and controlled repetitions
- Keep your torso stabilized and your upper body straight
- Lower yourself until your upper arms are parallel to the ground

AVOID
- Excessive speed
- Shallow or bouncy repetitions
- Overtaxing the shoulders

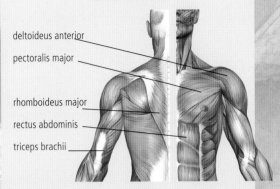

TARGET MUSCLES

deltoideus anterior
pectoralis major
rhomboideus major
rectus abdominis
triceps brachii

REAR   FRONT

TRICEPS

Swiss Ball Dumbbell Curls

Swiss Ball Dumbbell Curls are particularly effective for strengthening the biceps and, to a lesser extent, the forearms. By sitting on a Swiss ball while executing the curls, the routine also boosts strength in your core muscles.

Step 1 Begin seated on a Swiss ball holding a pair of dumbbells at arm's length by your sides.

Step 2 Slowly bend your elbows and lift up the dumbbells until they are up by your shoulders. Return to the starting position and complete 10 to 12 repetitions.

CORRECT ACTION
- Try to keep your shoulders relaxed through the routine
- Lower the dumbbells in a controlled manner

AVOID
- Building up too much speed
- Using your shoulders excessively

TARGET MUSCLES

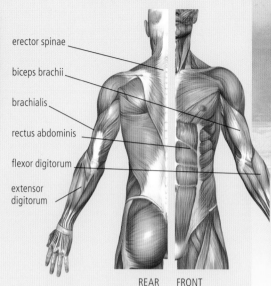

erector spinae

biceps brachii

brachialis

rectus abdominis

flexor digitorum

extensor digitorum

REAR   FRONT

BICEPS

Triangle Push-Ups with Medicine Ball

Triangle Push-Ups are even more taxing than standard push-ups, while incorporating a medicine ball into the exercise adds a further twist again. This is a highly effective routine for strengthening the triceps.

Step 1 Start in a facedown position on your toes—planted shoulder-width apart—with your hands on either side of a medicine ball, forming a triangle directly beneath your chest.

Step 2 Lower yourself until your upper arms are parallel to the ground and your chest almost touches the ball. Then push your arms to full extension.

Step 3 Keep your core engaged and your body straight as you lower again and continue for 12 to 15 repetitions.

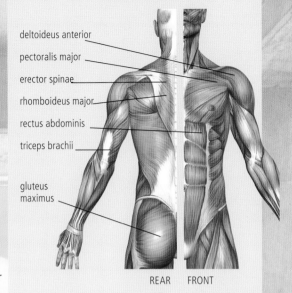

TARGET MUSCLES

deltoideus anterior
pectoralis major
erector spinae
rhomboideus major
rectus abdominis
triceps brachii

gluteus maximus

REAR   FRONT

TRICEPS

CORRECT ACTION
- Look for slow and controlled repetitions
- Keep your upper body straight
- Lower yourself until your upper arms are parallel to the ground

AVOID
- Excessive speed
- Shallow or bouncy repetitions
- Allowing the lower back to dip too far

Barbell Curls

The standard Barbell Curl has been around since the inception of strength training and is widely considered the granddaddy of biceps exercises for the ultimate in power and mass. A favorite in gyms across the globe, it is right up there with bench presses and sit-ups in terms of popularity.

Step 1 Pick up a barbell and let it hang at arm's length in front of you with a shoulder-width, underhand grip.

Step 2 Bend at the elbows until your palms are nearly touching your shoulders, then return to the starting position.

Step 3 Continue to complete 10 to 12 repetitions.

CORRECT ACTION
- Look for a full and complete range of motion
- Aim for proper body posture and alignment
- Strive for a controlled lowering of the weight

AVOID
- Swinging the weight upward
- Excessive speed or momentum
- Using your lower back excessively

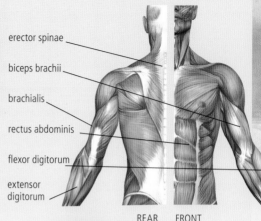

TARGET MUSCLES

erector spinae

biceps brachii

brachialis

rectus abdominis

flexor digitorum

extensor digitorum

REAR   FRONT

BICEPS

Bottoms-Up Kettlebell Clean

The Bottoms-Up Kettlebell Clean is a simple way of developing strength in the forearms, biceps, and shoulders.

Step 1 Stand upright, with your feet shoulder-width apart, holding a kettlebell in your right hand. Swing the kettlebell backward, then bring it forward and above your head forcefully, squeezing the handle as you do so.

Step 2 Once your upper arm is parallel to the floor, hold the position, then lower your arm again. Complete 8 to 10 repetitions before switching to the other arm.

CORRECT ACTION
- Keep your back straight throughout the movement

AVOID
- Adopting a loose grip

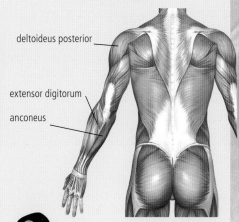

TARGET MUSCLES

deltoideus posterior

extensor digitorum

anconeus

FOREARMS

Reverse Close-Grip Front Chin

Though challenging, this classic pull-up routine delivers major strength benefits to the biceps and back muscles. You could get someone to support the weight of your legs or even place a dumbbell between your lower legs for increased resistance.

Step 1 Standing in front of a pull-up bar, either reach up or step on a stool. Take an underhand shoulder-width grip and hang below at arm's length.

Step 2 Cross your legs at the ankles, and pull yourself up.

Step 3 When your chin is as close to the bar as possible, lower yourself back to arm's length. Repeat 8 to 10 times.

TARGET MUSCLES

erector spinae

biceps brachii

rectus abdominis

flexor digitorum

extensor digitorum

REAR   FRONT

BICEPS

CORRECT ACTION
- Always perform a full range of motion

AVOID
- Dropping your body weight suddenly

Wide-Grip High Pull

The Wide-Grip High Pull works on the legs, upper back, forearms, and core to increase strength and mass in the upper body and thighs. Make the routine easier by using a lighter barbell, or add an extra degree of difficulty by moving your feet closer together.

Step 1 Stand in front of a barbell with your feet hip-width apart; your shins should be close to the bar.

Step 2 Bend your legs until your thighs are nearly parallel to the ground, then grab the barbell with a grip that is just beyond shoulder width.

Step 3 Keeping a flat back, straighten your knees to stand up, then pull the barbell up to your shoulders.

Step 4 Lower the barbell to arm's length and return it to the floor. Perform 8 to 10 repetitions.

CORRECT ACTION
• Always keep a flat back

AVOID
• Performing the exercise at excessive speed

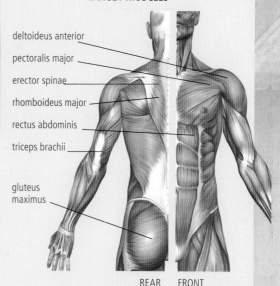

TARGET MUSCLES

deltoideus anterior
pectoralis major
erector spinae
rhomboideus major
rectus abdominis
triceps brachii
gluteus maximus

REAR   FRONT
UPPER BODY

2

3

Back Exercises

The back is responsible for pulling down from above, pulling back from in front, and hyperextending at the waist. It contains a complex series of muscles, including the latissimus dorsi (commonly known as the lats) and trapezius, that are second in size in the body only to the gluteus maximus. The back's powerful muscles are capable of generating incredible power and performance. Consistent, intelligent, and thorough back training will also result in an improved V-taper.

Incline Dumbbell Row

For those with lower-back pain or who lack the control required to maintain a flat back during exercise, the Incline Dumbbell Row is ideal. It takes the strain from the lower back and places stress on the correct muscles. You can use a Swiss ball or an incline bench for the routine.

Step 1 Begin by placing your upper body on a Swiss ball with your legs stretched out behind you and a pair of dumbbells in your hands.

Step 2 Move the dumbbells outward, contracting your lats hard as you do so.

Step 3 Lower the dumbbells back down to full extension and continue the exercise for 8 to 10 repetitions.

TARGET MUSCLES

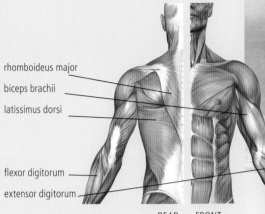

rhomboideus major

biceps brachii

latissimus dorsi

flexor digitorum

extensor digitorum

REAR   FRONT

BACK

CORRECT ACTION
- Maintain a flat back throughout the movement
- Contract each repetition at the top of the movement

AVOID
- Rounding your back
- Excessively swinging the weight
- Allowing the dumbbell to drop following the completion of each repetition

Standing Single-Arm Band Row

The Standing Single-Arm Band Row is a functional exercise in which the core plays almost as important a role as the lat muscles. As well as being a fantastic routine for the upper back, it is a lesson in stability and requires the various muscle groups to work together.

Step 1 Set one end of a band firmly in place at a low angle while holding the other end in your hand.

Step 2 Lean forward and stand in a staggered stance.

Step 3 Pull the handle toward your chest as you rotate your torso in the same direction.

Step 4 Contract, then return to the starting position and continue to complete 8 to 10 repetitions per side.

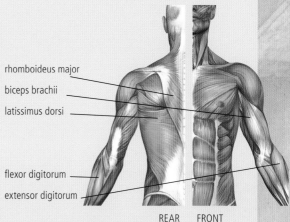

TARGET MUSCLES

rhomboideus major
biceps brachii
latissimus dorsi
flexor digitorum
extensor digitorum

REAR   FRONT
BACK

CORRECT ACTION
- Look for a flat back throughout
- Brace your core

AVOID
- Pulling too low on your abdomen
- Excessive speed or swing
- Using your arms too much instead of your back

EZ Bar Pullover

The EZ Bar Pullover is a classic routine that many associate with chest training. In reality, it is also highly effective for developing the serratus muscles as well as the latissimus dorsi that runs along the back. This exercise also differs from triceps extensions in that, though bent, the entire arm travels behind the head instead of just the forearms.

Step 1 Begin lying on a flat bench with your head supported and your legs bent, with both feet on the floor.

Step 2 Hold an EZ bar extended above your chest with your hands on the inside grooves.

Step 3 Start bending your arms back behind your head as you stretch throughout the torso, and then lengthen them as you rise back into the starting position for 8 to 10 repetitions.

TARGET MUSCLES

serratus

latissimus dorsi

rectus abdominis

triceps brachii

REAR   FRONT

BACK

CORRECT ACTION
• Keep your head on the bench at all times
• Be sure to stretch well behind your head
• Maintain a flat lower back throughout
  the movement

AVOID
• Arching your back
• Swinging the weight excessively
• Keeping your arms straight during the stretch

Hyperextension

Hyperextensions are excellent lower-back exercises. However, they need to be approached with care—you must ensure a proper range of motion and speed of execution.

Step 1 Assume a prone or facedown position on a bench with your thighs supported by the pads.

Step 2 Keeping your legs close together, cross your hands in front of your chest.

Step 3 Start by rising at the trunk until your body is in one straight line, flexing the glutes and lower back at the top of the movement. Lower and repeat for 12 to 15 repetitions.

CORRECT ACTION
- Look for a controlled raising
- Keep your body correctly situated for proper stabilization
- Contract each repetition at the top of the movement

AVOID
- Excessive body movement
- Keeping your legs too wide

TARGET MUSCLES

erector spinae

gluteus maximus

biceps femoris

REAR   FRONT

BACK

Twisting Hyperextension

The Twisting Hyperextension is an advanced version of the Hyperextension that strengthens the entire core, not just the lower back. As with the traditional Hyperextension exercise, caution is required with regards to execution and speed.

Step 1 Asume a prone or facedown position on a bench with your thighs supported by the pads.

Step 2 Keeping your legs close together, place your fingers on your ears with your elbows flared outward.

Step 3 Raise your body at the trunk and rotate to the left at the waist.

Step 4 Lower yourself and rise back up, this time in the opposite direction. Complete 6 to 8 repetitions per side.

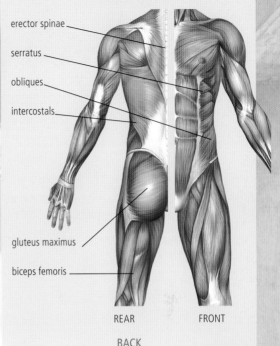

TARGET MUSCLES

- erector spinae
- serratus
- obliques
- intercostals
- gluteus maximus
- biceps femoris

REAR FRONT

BACK

CORRECT ACTION
- Look for a controlled raising
- Aim for a precise twist
- Contract each repetition at the top of the movement

AVOID
- Hyperextending too high
- Excessive body movement
- Keeping your legs too wide

Kettlebell Double Row

The Kettlebell Double Row is a very effective strengthening exercise for the upper back. It also works the stabilizing muscles of the upper body. Take care to execute the motion with a flat back, total control, and proper speed of movement.

Step 1 Stand up straight with a pair of kettlebells in your hands.

Step 2 Bend forward at the waist while maintaining a flat back. Bend the knees slightly and stick your rear out.

Step 3 Pull the kettlebells up toward your chest, contracting the lats hard as you do so.

Step 4 Lower the kettlebells back down to full extension and continue for 8 to 10 repetitions.

TARGET MUSCLES

- trapezius
- deltoideus posterior
- rhomboideus major
- biceps brachii
- latissimus dorsi
- erector spinae
- multifidus spinae
- flexor digitorum
- extensor digitorum

REAR   FRONT

BACK

CORRECT ACTION
- Maintain a flat back throughout the movement
- Pull next to your chest, not your shoulders
- Contract each repetition at the top of the movement

AVOID
- Rounding your back
- Excessively swinging the weight
- Allowing the kettlebells to drop following the completion of each repetition

2   3   4

Alternating Kettlebell Row

The Alternating Kettlebell Row builds strength in the middle back. It also benefits the biceps and latissimus dorsi. You can make the exercise less challenging by lifting with both arms at the same time, or more difficult by raising one leg off the floor.

Step 1 Stand upright with your feet shoulder-width apart. Hold a pair of kettlebells in front of you with an overhand grip. Bend forward slightly at the waist, maintaining a flat back.

Step 2 Bend your arm at the elbow, and pull your right hand up toward your abdomen, then lower it again.

Step 3 Next, pull your left hand up, then lower it. Complete 8 to 10 repetitions per hand.

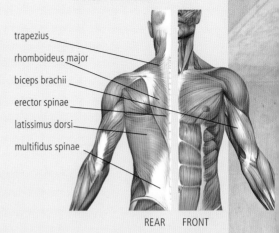

TARGET MUSCLES

trapezius
rhomboideus major
biceps brachii
erector spinae
latissimus dorsi
multifidus spinae

REAR   FRONT

BACK

CORRECT ACTION
• Maintain a flat back during the exercise

AVOID
• Rotating your core

Alternating Renegade Row

Another great routine for the middle back, the Alternating Renegade Row also strengthens the abdominals, biceps, chest, latissimus dorsi, and triceps.

Step 1 With a kettlebell in each hand, place yourself on the floor in a push-up position.

Step 2 While still up on your toes—and keeping your core stable and parallel to the floor—pull the kettlebell in your right hand up toward your chest. At the same time, straighten your left arm and push that kettlebell into the floor.

Step 3 Lower your right arm, then repeat the movement with your left arm. Complete 8 to 10 repetitions per arm.

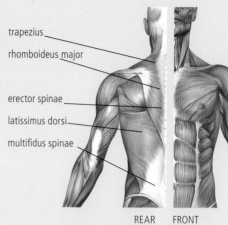

TARGET MUSCLES

trapezius
rhomboideus major
erector spinae
latissimus dorsi
multifidus spinae

REAR   FRONT

BACK

CORRECT ACTION
• Keep your core stable and straight

AVOID
• Dropping or slamming the weight into the floor

Band Pull-Apart

The Band Pull-Apart is a simple routine that targets the middle back, trapezius, and shoulders. It is a straightforward way of increasing strength and mass in your shoulders.

Step 1 Stand with your feet shoulder-width apart, holding a band straight out in front of you. Your hands should also be shoulder-width apart.

Step 2 Perform a fly motion, pulling the band across your chest and out to the sides, while keeping your palms facing down. Pause for a moment, then return to the starting position. Repeat 10 to 15 times.

TARGET MUSCLES

deltoideus anterior
infraspinatus
supraspinatus
subscapularis
deltoideus medialis
deltoideus posterior
teres major
teres minor

REAR   FRONT

BACK

CORRECT ACTION
• Keep your shoulders back

AVOID
• Being carried by momentum

Barbell Deadlift

The Barbell Deadlift increases power and mass in the torso. It benefits a wide range of muscles, including the erector spinae, quads, glutes, hamstrings, and biceps, as well as the core and forearms. An easier approach is to use a lighter bar or just your own body weight; alternatively, bring your feet closer together, which increases the range of motion required.

Step 1 Begin by standing with your feet shoulder-width apart in front of a barbell. Looking straight ahead, squat down and grab the barbell with a wide overhand grip; make sure your knees are close to the bar.

Step 2 Push through your heels as you stand erect while holding the barbell below you, at arm's length. Be sure to keep a straight back throughout this movement.

Step 3 Stand fully erect while holding the completed movement, then carefully lower the barbell to the ground. Perform 6 to 8 repetitions.

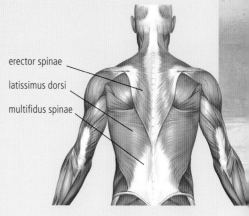

TARGET MUSCLES

erector spinae

latissimus dorsi

multifidus spinae

BACK

CORRECT ACTION
• Use your glutes to help with the movement

AVOID
• Overarching your back

1

2

3

Barbell Power Clean and Jerk

The classic Barbell Power Clean and Jerk boosts power and mass in the shoulders and upper back, especially the deltoids and triceps. It also benefits the thighs, glutes, hamstrings, and core. Vary the difficulty levels by using dumbbells instead of a barbell, or a very light bar.

Step 1 Stand in front of a barbell with your feet should shoulder-width apart. Squat down and grab the barbell with a wide overhand grip.

Step 2 As you return to a standing position, flip the barbell until it is nearly touching your upper chest.

Step 3 Next, push the barbell overhead, holding it at arm's length.

Step 4 Lower the barbell back to your upper chest, reverse your flip, and return it to the floor. Perform 6 to 8 repetitions.

TARGET MUSCLES

deltoideus anterior
infraspinatus
supraspinatus
teres major
deltoideus medialis
deltoideus posterior
erector spinae
triceps brachii

REAR   FRONT

SHOULDERS AND TRICEPS

CORRECT ACTION
• Be sure to use your legs to help with the start of the movement

AVOID
• Overarching your back

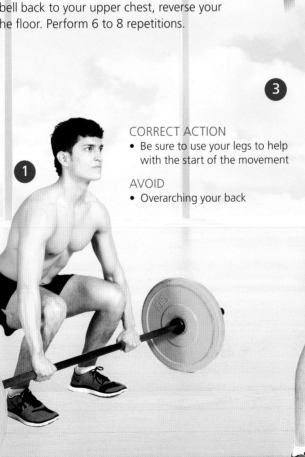

Lat Pulldowns

Lat Pulldowns focus on the latissimus dorsi, forearms, and biceps, increasing strength and width in the back muscles. A wider grip makes for an easier routine as it reduces your range of motion, while a closer grip does the opposite and so makes it more of a challenge.

Step 1 Begin in a seated position at a pulldown machine. Grab the bar with an overhand grip that is slightly wider than shoulder width.

Step 2 Pull the bar down to the very top of your chest.

Step 3 Fully extend your arms overhead using a controlled movement. Complete 8 to 10 repetitions.

CORRECT ACTION
• Always sit up straight, maintaining a flat back

AVOID
• Pulling the bar behind your neck

TARGET MUSCLES

deltoideus posterior

latissimus dorsi

brachioradialis

extensor digitorum

BACK

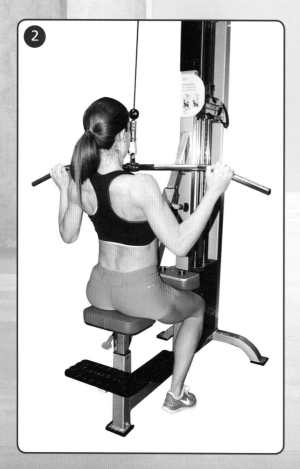

Barbell Upright Rows

Barbell Upright Rows increase power and mass in the trapezius muscles. They also target the front deltoids, upper back, forearms, biceps, and core. Swap the barbell for a very light bar to make the routine less challenging.

Step 1 Pick up a barbell with a relatively close grip and let it hang at arms' length in front of you.

Step 2 Keeping your body erect, pull the barbell straight up.

Step 3 When the barbell is nearly touching your chin, lower it back to arm's length. Repeat 10 to 12 times.

CORRECT ACTION
- Always keep the barbell close to your body
- Lead with your elbows

AVOID
- Hitting your chin with the barbell

TARGET MUSCLES

deltoideus anterior

trapezius

biceps brachii

REAR   FRONT

TRAPEZIUS

Workouts

These thematic workouts take into account the differing goals and parameters one reading this book might have. Ranging in scope and intensity, they are thorough and challenging, and are great examples of how to put exercises together in terms of chasing and achieving one's goal in a linear manner. Be safe, take your time, and above all, have fun.

Beginner Workout

Suitable for all levels, especially those new to strength training.

1 Barbell Bench Press, p. 84

2 Swiss Ball Dumbbell Fly, p. 80

5 Dumbbell Shoulder Press, p. 97

6 Barbell Curls, p. 126

8 Barbell Squats, p. 30

9 Lying Leg Curls, p. 25

3 Lat Pulldowns, p. 144

4 Barbell Deadlift, p. 142

7 Assisted Dips, p. 120

10 Standing Calf Raise, p. 51

Upper-Body Workout

Specializing in strengthening the major muscles of the upper body.

1 Swiss Ball Incline Dumbbell Press, p. 78

2 Swiss Ball Dumbbell Fly, p. 80

8 Swiss Ball Dumbbell Curls, p. 124

5 Wide-Grip High Pull, p. 129

9 Dumbbell Shrug, p. 104

3 Decline Push-Up, p. 82

4 EZ Bar Pullover, p. 134

7 Dumbbell Power Clean and Press, p. 94

6 Kettlebell Double-Row, p. 138

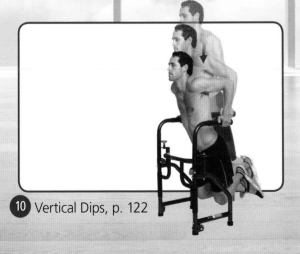

10 Vertical Dips, p. 122

Lower-Body Workout

Specializing in strengthening the major muscles of the lower body.

1 Kettlebell Figure-Eight, p. 26

2 Hack Squats, p. 32

5 One-Legged Extension, p. 34

6 Seated Leg Curls, p. 24

9 Standing Calf Raise, p. 51

10 Mountain Climber, p. 48

3 Goblet Squat, p. 45

4 Reverse Lunge, p. 50

7 Lying Leg Curls, p. 25

8 Barbell Deadlift, p. 142

Performance Workout

Specializing in improving explosive strength and power.

1 Perfect Push-Up, p. 81

2 Plyo Kettlebell Push-Up, p. 88

5 Hyperextension, p. 136

6 Barbell Deadlift, p. 142

9 Lying Leg Curls, p. 25

10 Seated Calf Raise, p. 52

3 EZ Bar Pullover, p. 134

4 Reverse Close-Grip Front Chin, p. 128

7 Kettlebell Double-Clean, p. 96

8 Barbell Squats, p. 30

Body-Weight Workout

Specializing in strengthening the overall body on its own merits without the use of additional resistance.

1 Burpees, p. 41

2 Perfect Push-Up, p. 81

5 Sit-Ups, p. 56

9 Vertical Dips, p. 122

8 Twisting Hyperextension, p. 137

3 Decline Push-Up, p. 82

4 Plyo Kettlebell Push-Up, p. 88

6 Lateral Low Lunge, p. 36

7 Hyperextension, p. 136

10 Plyometric Push-Up, p. 90

Kamikaze Workout

For the ultimate in training intensity and challenge.

1 Swiss Ball Dumbbell Fly, p. 80

2 Plyo Kettlebell Push-Up, p. 88

5 Barbell Deadlift, p. 142

6 Bottoms-Up Kettlebell Clean, p. 127

9 Barbell Squats, p. 30

10 Box Jumps, p. 40

3 Reverse Close-Grip Front Chin, p. 128

4 Twisting Hyperextension, p. 137

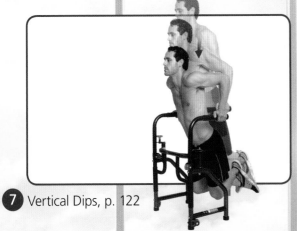

7 Vertical Dips, p. 122

8 Plyometric Push-Up, p. 90

Acknowledgments

Photography

Photography by Jonathan Conklin

www.jonathanconklin.net

Illustrations

All illustrations by by Shutterstock/Linda Bucklin.

Acknowledgments

The author offers thanks to those closely involved in the creation of this book: Moseley Road art director Tina Vaughan, editorial director Damien Moore, editor Phil Hunt, designer Heather McCarry, and production director Adam Moore.

About the author

Hollis Lance Liebman has been a fitness magazine editor, national bodybuilding champion, and author. He is a published physique photographer and has served as a bodybuilding and fitness competition judge.

Visit his Web site, www.holliswashere.com, for fitness tips and complete training programs. This is his fourth book.